I0709354

On a public bus journey speeding down a mountain jungle dirt road
deep into the night, practically all night, the most afraid I'd ever
been—bouncing around, swerving, unbelted, front seat, cracked
windshield, debris-covered face, blown tire, skidding to a halt,
changed tire, a gentleman of these lands put his hand on my thigh
and piercing my eyes in a comforting way gave me this...

"It's good to experience the road"
— Pondo, Papua New Guinea, 2016

Cofounders: Taj Forer and Michael Itkoff
Creative Director: Ursula Damm
Copy Editor: Gabrielle Fastman

ISBN: 978-1-954119-17-8

Printed by Ofset Yapimevi, Turkey

Daylight Books
E-mail: info@daylightbooks.org
Web: www.daylightbooks.org

A Sum of One

Derek Schrock

Daylight

*For anyone who welcomed a stranger's journey
through their door and to their table.
And for my parents, whom I love beyond measure.*

FOREWORD

by Dan Friend

All of my adult life I have been involved with photography in one way or another. This interest of mine started as a hobby that developed into a career that lasted forty-five years. I started my own studio many years ago and worked up from those beginnings to my current livelihood of making fine art photography. A career in photography has even allowed me to give back to the medium, as well as my alma mater, by retiring as manager of the West Virginia University photography department.

The interesting thing about photography is, as you start photographing, you start discovering things about yourself. Most people take pictures of things they like or love. Parents take thousands of pictures of their children, their spouses, and friends having fun. Why? Because those are things that are important to them, things they care about. Some people take this a step further and go beyond the family vacation and children's photos. They use photography to observe the world around them, and at the same time, observe themselves.

As a person grows with their photography, they want to learn, see, and have life experiences they capture with their camera. The photographer is really learning more about what their likes and dislikes are, what they are enthusiastic about, what grabs their interests and talks to their inner self. It becomes a process of self-discovery.

Derek started off with a love of travel. He took the camera along at first just to record his adventures. He did not start off as a professional photographer, but his love of travel, people, and faraway places started to take on a different meaning because of photography. As his photographic skills increased, he discovered the importance of creating visual images. Composition, light, exposure, mood, and capturing the moment can convey feelings in a way the written word cannot. He became aware that his photography was not just about documenting his trips—it was becoming a way to express himself. Derek's photos started to tell of the personal journey he was on. He started painting with his images to help tell that story.

You will enjoy the beautiful landscapes and exotic places documented here, but I think you will get the true meaning of the book while looking at the portraits of people and the candid images of them living their lives in these faraway places. One portrait series thoughtfully conveys the love a father has for his son, while the individual portrait series captures its subjects' stories exceptionally well and reminds us we are all "a sum of one."

SHAPING MY NATURE FROM NATURE

by Derek Schrock

My photographs are an expression of my existence. Being present, I went to the ends of the earth to see again. I took a journey abroad, beyond my grounds, mapping my soul as a constellation belonging to me, Derek Schrock, owner of one. My name, my soul, had become misplaced—I couldn't capture, describe, nor recognize them. Unbeknownst to me, being aware of this was to become my greatest fortune. Recognizing that I could reclaim myself was clearly a golden opportunity. The existence of a deep void enveloped me in a dark shadow, propelling me forward on this journey abroad, which exposed an opposing flash of light that illuminated my reawakening. The sowing of my soul, by an arrangement of places traveled, was my ultimate investment. Figuratively, this was my natural burial to bid farewell to a lost self.

Unfulfilled by the road taken, I strapped on a backpack to trek across six continents and encountered sheltering embraces that mended my being. The wild landscapes, happening streets, and endearing faces in some of the most remote places in the world contained a cultural significance that served as the influential callings, contrasts, and medicine in which I found myself.

This is neither a heroic story of accomplishment nor a sad story of a broken soul. I am not a summiting alpinist or hopeless wanderer. The adventure was never about the pinnacles hit from ascension or the descending to accolades upon return. Forged in an athletic background, ambitions of winning awards to justify my efforts had been shed. Those dreams expired. It was about the journey and how it happened. The immersion of an experience into something spiritual. To rethink what it means to be a witness to the lives of others and to contemplate how far we are or are not from one another, in a great many things. More than anything this is a thank-you for the gift of this journey. Complications unfolded before me, as the road was an ironing of the soul. But it was easier than expected, like meeting the love of your life and feeling a particular way and not having to explain it.

Life is simplified on a big adventure. The checklist is short on an existential walk. A North Star, self-determination, a back, and a pack. Searching is innate and the weight of the pack to the back demands the necessity of self. The further I went, the lighter the pack got. Yes, my conditioning upgraded, and I learned to pack better, but additionally, the further I went the more I was given. New callings were revealed, with new directions answering those calls to address the idiosyncrasies of my nature and place them in the profound enormity of the world that was created in my classic years. There's nowhere I would have rather been, no position in professional attire I would have rather held. I wasn't climbing any career ladder. This was it for me. And it became my work.

A family vacation gifted to the Schrocks to a divided Germany in the eighties certainly planted a seed. I remember feeling a sense of adventure at the age of five. Then there was the Christmas gift of a globe, which I would spin endlessly. A passion for maps and hunger for novel spaces, there was a fire lit inside of me to explore the great unknown. My father once pinned a quote by Henry David Thoreau: "If one advances confidently in the direction of his dreams, and endeavors to live a life in which he has imagined, he will meet with a success unexpected in common hours." I wasn't sure what it meant for the longest time; blind to it, I did pull-ups in front of it. Somehow, it rubbed off. I followed my dreams, from once being static to being in the eye of pulsating light, and there my dreams had the geometry of beautiful lines and shapes. I went with all I had, with the hope of becoming a better person, more rounded and one with my surroundings. Plus, traveling is romantic and who wouldn't do it if they could?

I traveled with my flaws and faults, found my strengths, and learned I was capable. A modern-day hunter and gatherer of the soul, I passionately sought my unknown while remaining in an attractive state of anonymity, illuminated by the intimate understanding I so valued—all with a camera present and focus to balance. I went alone and cut off; there were no tagging posts. I was traveling in a pure style. Not knowing initially what I had been about, just going with a heart on full tilt, I photographed the world I saw with gut instinct. I took up photography as a means of companionship, to overcome my tendency of being closed off, while wandering to far-reaching lengths. As an elongated form of self, photography was a means to communicatively engage and not be alone. As it turns out, I was never alone.

My parents always gave me the absolute best of their love and wholeheartedly believed in me. That became our clash because I wasn't sure how I felt about myself. Self-doubt flooded my existence. My life was "treading water," devoid of purpose or passion. Consequently, stuck in nearsightedness, the fortitude of my spirit was weak. I had retreated deep inside, lost and torn, and the worry persisted that I wasn't coming back. To not seek is utterly disorienting. I loved my parents too much to stay in that state. The system wasn't for me. Working a nine-to-five job and packing it in wasn't for me. I belonged in a different time, a different place, and neither were scheduled around ball games and beach holidays. Guilty of being a good soldier of society, I conformed and followed its charted path right up to the edge of being fake. But then I jumped.

Association sharpens sight and I did not associate in my surroundings; I had become desensitized. I wasn't ready to settle upon being franchised. I wasn't a mold. I was unfinished and out of light. My skin needed to shed. Converting a paycheck into a plane ticket to a place most folks haven't heard of definitely raises eyebrows and invites alienating remarks. I would be positioned in the wrong, but never felt so very right. I became proud of believing in things, places, and people that others overlooked. I finally had it, an equal and opposing reaction, and it was going to propel me across the world.

From urban and otherworldly landscapes to life in secluded villages, I was on a path of discovery that was good for me. The progression of travel was innate. The simplicity of my evolution was printing a passport photograph, purchasing a backpack, a plane ticket, marking maps with a Sharpie, dipping my toes on the rails of Europe, and exiting to collect tickets and see tourist sites. I wore that backpack to the bone. I traversed Swiss glaciers, walked the streets of Rome in the middle of the night having the shadows of the Colosseum to myself, strapped a pack on the back for kilometers to a central station, then on to airports where I slept on that backpack. The Europe I saw was storybook and comforting to my soul. All I saw, I recognized. I was pleased and proud; it was a nice escalation. It made me feel better, but not be better. The method of travel was not challenging, nor did it aid in developing the soul. Alteration doesn't happen by hanging wall calendars or booking vacation spots. I identified elsewhere. I love and appreciate those initial travels; they certainly planted a seed. Eventually though, the seed blossomed into a question: Are you a traveler, or are you a tourist? A backpacker could be either.

The world is diverse across a large spectrum. Quickly composing a sentence of what comprises this world becomes a sentence without end. As with the sky, it's a multi-faceted arrangement with pitches and arcs, patterns with and without edges, and countless intensities and complexities. Bits and pieces contributed by everyone and everything, across everywhere. Would I witness as much of that composition as I could? Stay for as long as I could? As this composition is ever changing, articulated by many, I didn't want just one point of view or a single voice.

A well-balanced perspective of the world holds the views of many. The more views I observed, the more I wanted to listen and the better bearings I kept. The most beautiful mother in the world tells her son she's only upset with him when he's not being a good listener. I wanted to kneel next to a river sourced from the voices of nature and drink under their guardianship. I wanted to be a traveler.

I would go as many places as I could and as far as I could. The further I went, the closer I got to myself. I saw the world, overcame mental barriers, and wasn't terrified. I was inspired by what was to follow. Sure, I'd wake up in the middle of the night with sweats, boiling points of anxiety, and think to myself, What am I doing? Call it wisdom, call it foolishness. I took it as a nod of reassurance that I was experiencing the road and it was incredibly good for me. Some of it was a beating and I'd whisper "uncle," but I was hitched to seeing the world and the style in which I was seeing it. I always came back for more. Enamored by all of it, the road taken and the way in which I chose to explore it. Engaging, challenging, and intimate travel without glamour. I was in it, picking up influence under natural elements. A signature with sincerity. Each time I headed out I was met with certain trials. Blisters from the sweltering heat, blisters from walking the road, intense humidity and rain-soaked clothes, bone-crushing glacial ice, sagging shoulder blades, torn blue jeans covered in dirt, mosquito bites, face wounds from dust storms, and weight loss. Entering the space of others, I accept I'm the least knowledgeable, the minority, and on trial. New methods of eating and a shower earned over days were warmly welcomed.

Just don't give me air-conditioning, television, or the availability of a cell phone.

With my phone on airplane mode over a range of continents (Asia, Africa, Australia, and South America) and seated over the wing of a plane, I knew there was nowhere I'd rather be. Cruising altitude was my meditative state. Mountains merging with jungle from desert to savannah and coastline again. I had become a traveler! I was a bird touching down with striking talons on a modest airstrip and when the hatch opened, I could feel the air sail into my lungs. I never felt so alive. So glad to be in a certain place, wherever that place may be. In this method of travel, in surrounding myself entirely in the unknown, it became a sensory experience. Lighthouses to the human spirit, these flashes cast infinitely and illuminated my path in the dark corridors of my soul. I knew I would find my way.

Echoing the human heart on the whispers of others, I learned of myself through flourishes of humanity. I may not have understood their spoken word, but I felt its weight in translation by guide, pitch, tone, ambience of articulation, and the silences between sound. I learned what was important in where I was. A shaman in the mountains of Colombia tied himself to me in a bracelet placed around my wrist upon a trek, accompanied by his spoken words. Stories that were shared at a tribal gathering in Angola around a fire burning all night and resupplied all day kept me warm. Warmer by the fact that I contributed to the fire. Then there was the swinging of a machete against the dense interior of Papua New Guinea to carve out a safe place to listen to birds of paradise before the sun came up; the birds sang, and I stayed for the performance from beginning to end. I was indeed learning different languages and what it meant to listen. What I heard shaped me, altered my programming. I spoke back. After a performance via translator in the Simbu province in the mountains of Papua New Guinea, I expressed my appreciation for being accepted into their world through eye contact and handshakes. This welcoming was admirable and injected in me a sense of calm. A conversation of peace in one part of the world happens all over the world. This is true of any conversation on any traveled path. In traveling, the dots at the end of sentences connect to map the world. Listening abroad becomes a conversation on the layover and then domestically. A responsibility of being a traveler is carrying messages. Some are lighter than others. When you travel up close you become involved. You care more. You're willing to put your emotions on the rocks, because in these moments, you meet others halfway.

Peace has a place. In Japan, presiding over the Children's Peace Monument are the voices of schoolchildren reciting words about the atomic atrocities in Hiroshima in 1945. Peace, love, hope, and healing during challenging times shape the accompanying paper cranes. Getting close to the folds of others helps me with my own. On Uganda's most northern edge, lions escaped my sight by day, but by night, one by one, they roared parallel with shooting stars. I slept under them, tucked in truce. I listened.

In my own element, I had never been spiritual, but being on location changed me, made me vulnerable to the impression of others. They could put their stamp on me however they wanted to. The significance of going solo is to be swallowed by others. I wasn't in a cocoon. No creature comforts. I ate where I was in the manner food was to be eaten. The meals were not my right, but a gift from one life to another.

Dangling my feet from a rooftop edge in a blacked-out Myanmar city, I found a love for beef Stroganoff. Every time I've had it since, I remember the ensemble of curious waiters and waitresses giving me the plate and fork. I was their only customer in a heavily unvisited country. A Tokyo chef, with hands reminiscent of what I saw in Michelangelo's *David*, gave me sushi and it changed my life. A dinner among strangers in southern Ethiopia from a shared plate, using injera to scoop up the food with bare hands. Veggies, meat, or raw meat. It didn't matter. To react to injera is to feel better about a great many things. I was in the company of others and loved it, and their influence blossomed flavorful on my tastebuds.

Traveling isn't all romantic, however. Caught in a rainstorm with hours to dry, I was cold and shivering. Weak, beaten, and bruised, I lost a shoe from a wrong place, wrong time scenario and found myself for the first and only time on the wrong end of a fight. I needed it. A rainstorm and rolling are opposite ends of the spectrum, and in between were plenty of barriers to overcome. Though, I never got an upset stomach or ill. Not once. I was close once in Ecuador, brought on by natural causes, but a lady of a homestead took some plants from her forest and made

me tea. It was lovely. No meal from another ever did any harm. They only gave me the comfort I needed, when I needed it, restoring my motivation. I'll never forget ordering dinner one late night in Ethiopia from a restaurant with no menu. I placed an order, and shortly thereafter, a boy left the kitchen with a machete. It was the best meal I ever had. If you'd like to know, it was buttered goat with a side of fresh bread.

Smelling salts to a concussion, these were the aromas I would wake to on the road. Planted, personalized, and presented under my nose. Chili peppers in a sack on the floor of a market while spices sat upright in abundance. Pillars of spice. African markets have an abundance of supplies. Any scent imaginable was for the taking and they all messaged, "Wake up." Coffee could be found, uncommercialized, around every turn. Side-street coffee tents across Africa to a plantation in Colombia to a modern Bangkok coffee house trace back to walking the coffee aisle in the grocery store as a child alone to smell those fragrant beans. Many years later I was being ground.

Brighter than I've ever seen it, the sun peaked over New Zealand mountains illuminating a snowcapped lunar landscape. Since the dawn, landscapes have been a whetstone for humanity. Hiking has been an instrument for travel, and when it's good, it's like ballet. The placement of steps. Movement in ascent of high altitudes to descend upon civilizations is a humble experience in fragility. Keeping the lateral wits, just as important, to a balancing act. The fishermen on Inle Lake, Myanmar, fish their particular way with toes propelling and balancing the boat—a gray axis of art and survival.

Beneath the water's surface, sharks and stingrays swim the pathways of Australia, grazing a diver. Seeing a shark's eyes in person elicits a skipped heartbeat. Then there's bull jumping in southern Ethiopia. A boy's initiation carried out on the backs of cherished cattle into a life of love, ownership, and extending one's bloodline.

Much of life is a race, but awareness comes in slow forms too. Particularly under the guidance of a master. In complete stillness, a calming peace of mind, practicing Zen meditation in Kyoto. I gave it a go. In a quite different experience, situated in a stilt home on the banks of the Sepik River, I watched passing villagers trading tobacco in the middle of the night while negotiating next to a fire. This was my therapy couch and answer to the question, Who do you talk to about what's going on with you? Under a shelter of beams cut from species of grace and mercy, these were my discovered whereabouts.

I've slept plenty of nights sheeted one inch above the raw earth on my bristle pad. Touching the earth is cleansing. Be it soil, a lagoon, or showering under a shared waterfall, you shed your skin and take on new forms that become a part of you. And when it's good, you pass it forward.

A simple act can become a nation and one at the forefront of my mind is the gesture of shaking hands in Papua New Guinea. I've never seen it nor experienced it at such a genuine level. Morning, day, and night it's always given and received. Neighbor, traveler, son. Several times a day. In a steadying fashion, as a unique bond. In a culture where one lost soul shames us all, this touching act keeps a community tight between greetings and salutations and the eventuality of a farewell. It's in this signature sign of respect, from a gesture of esteemed peace and love, that I felt like one of their own from the moment I landed in a remote coastal town. Truly, I felt at home. An unwritten custom of their culture, the shaking of hands, is an invaluable relic of place. One I don't need to hoard, frame, display on a mantle and protect with my life. I can give it away every day for the rest of my life. Beautiful souls living in the mountains of Papua New Guinea or along the waters of the country's Sepik River. Many may have never had the opportunity—or desire—to travel to Scandinavia, Lisbon, Angola, or Colombia, but I did. And because I did after encountering them, they shook those places too.

My experiences finally brought life into focus. Diagnosed with glaucoma at an age much younger than one normally would be, I took it hard. I approached the diagnosis in a way more contemplative than medical. Was my sight impaired or was it all in my head in the denying of sight? My symptoms supported the former. Much of my traveling was to see clearly from the inside out. I imagined my eyes fully open, screaming to be stimulated and not being able to see. Would I freak? Did I have enough memories to flash before me for a lifetime? Rather than a weakness, could the optic nerve become unbreakable by traveling light?

Traveling gave me the depth of field to see myself in a whole new light. How things lie with me. What triggers happiness in me. What moves me to compassion and empathy. What leaves me speechless in awe's opposing dimensions of wonder and fear. How I'm an expert of nothing and with that nothingness I have the complete freedom to evolve and change through the power of taking risks. Listing what I care about, then taking a machete to the list and leaving intact what I really care about in this world. Through travel, I was getting to know a stranger. All it would take would be one focal rotation that clicks from one beacon of light. I received thousands.

The story of the iris is really the story of us. The more patterns of iris I saw in others, the more I recognized mine. Everyone knows it: the eyes are the window to the soul. We all say it. My reflection had never been so clear as it had been in the eyes of others until I didn't have to look anymore. I had fully found my bearings. In touch with my humanity, I looked at others with all my vision and the surroundings of their view. The goal of these journeys was self-discovery, a reawakening of my spirit, but I found something far more meaningful in surrounding myself in their world.

I never kept tally marks of places traveled while it was happening. I wasn't trailblazing a first ascent. What I did was go to a wide range of places and take in the perspective under a vast variety of influences. I've been to Berlin, Varanasi, Johannesburg, Medellín—together, a rare combination. I added to this scope by going to St. Petersburg, Geiranger, Nara, Teyuna, Kaminimbit, and Kidepo. Others have been, but not to each one, I'm guessing. Switching out one of mine for one of theirs. We move about the world placing ourselves momentarily, before migrating again. When invisible lines connect the dots of places we have been, it creates a special arrangement. Unique as a constellation and only drawn once in the

shape of one. No two people see the world the same way and no one person sees all the world. Collectively, the world is seen. This is what I saw.

Beauty has no bounds. It can be anywhere, inside anyone, and found in any circumstance to be projected endlessly. In the majestic landscape of Angola, beneath the argyle mountains and on the desert rocks of the Nguendelengo, there's a woman as beautiful as anyone in the world. She is bright, strong, and healthy. This beauty lives in a hut built by her family, made from branches, and the walls are crushed to little pieces then weaved into her hair, forming the uniqueness of her bun. A ring of bright-red-ochre paint from the earth encircles her neck and shoulders connecting her to her lands. The ring is priceless, eternal, and painted in love. In another part of the African continent, I walked the motorcycle-ridden dirt streets of a small tribal town in Ethiopia. A teen boy of Mursi descent, a son of his father, stood unbreakable from a spine forged over fire by the history of a bloodline. An able blacksmith couldn't hammer out anything stronger. The immaculacy of his posture bled to his strong gaze. Eyes of which commanded my full attention. What an honor, through my eyes and to my heart, his reflection ingrained in me while I reflected upon a reflection of me on the surface of his eyes. There I was because of him. Seeing is not a solitary endeavor and witnessing beauty under the forces of dignity was to remember what it was like to be spirited.

In Mingun, a face protected by a pale-yellow paste smeared in lines upon which the sentences of hopes and dreams could be written. Above the paste and in the eyes, I saw a longing for otherness. Plenty was to be written from belief in self-determination. A girl diving all the way down to the ocean floor off the Great Barrier Reef cocooned in a school of fish to overcome her fear of sharks. Way down at the bottom, she saw into the shark's eye and with a thumbs-up seemed better for it. Far away in another hemisphere, in Bogotá, another girl of similar age walked in heels, carrying a tote, and sporting jammed earbuds as she passed sprays, colors, and messaging in the urban block meccas of graffiti. I saw her response to the noise as to where it belongs, that being on the outside.

Rising from the male-dominated waters of Papua New Guinea's Sepik River, the crocodile is a historic source of reverence. Initiation into the spirit house only welcomes the spirit faces of one sex. Spirit houses are the ancestral lairs and modern dens where the spirits reside, and men of privilege guard the status quo. The scarification of the skin, symbolic of this triumphant initiation, bleeds as a stitch amongst a community preserving the garden of their view. The cuts of the skin usually aren't many, just enough to turn a boy into a man. Against the current I had decided to travel, and a woman of rebellious embrace didn't let her water's current veil the spirit of her face. The culmination of my travels emerged on a river's edge, in the crevasse of a rock face and backlit by the seals of fissures giving me this witnessing moment—the most powerful representation encountered on the Sepik was her, as she bled more than anyone else.

But nothing resonated with me more than the beautiful father and son of the Sepik River. Upriver, downriver, together we captained a boat. Papua New Guinea's vascularity runs deep and true. We launched from a mud bank in a dugout canoe. Sometimes the waters raged. Other times the tide ran extremely low, which meant you had to get your feet in the mud and push by hand in these crocodile-infested waters. Everyone contributed. Plenty of newcomers boarded then departed; to us it was a community vessel that kept us afloat. The father referred to the boy as "my little brother." "Here your little brother, Derek!" the father said, tossing him into my arms from the village's riverbank before pushing off again. My little brother had been unwell from a bacterial disease. I filtered the river's water and we navigated our way to the regional clinic. He ate the biggest portions sourced from the river to aid in his recovery. Nursing the boy back to himself, healing properties derived from the river, I slept with one eye open contemplating my two bunkmates against the night sounds of the Sepik. The love of a father and son. A son's will to not let go. When the father held up a flower to me and said, "You are this flower," I could trace the pinnacle of my travels back to my father. In this father and son, I saw us.

In 2015 I bought a delicacy in a Tokyo market from a kind face. I ate how a backpacker eats—exhausted, alone, feet up, and falling asleep. In 2018, I circled back, on the tail end of a trip's path that took me around the world. I was tired and weak with a very slim waist. I wandered to the same stall in a maze of stalls, just to see if she was still there. She was! There in that moment, seeing her, I was without words. Only feeling. Heart to eye. Swollen to a warm tear.

I always felt the weight of privilege upon what I had witnessed. And I was better for having seen it. Traveling was cathartic and photography set the keystone into shapes of images that became a part of me. I look at them as autobiographical. The world is loud and articulate and I was quiet and inarticulate. As the world made its impression on me, I observed and channeled it from the confines of a shadow. The best work I'll ever do on myself is this, these travels, under opposing flashes of light in the realms of others. An expression of one contributed by many. Over and over, trip after trip, decisive moments were assembled from sheer fate to fill an empty space. The silver lining of living in the shadows is that you can work things out free of judgment confronting the self-doubt on your own terms. And just when you're ready, at that very moment the light overtakes the shadow framing the instinctual click, from the inside out. Undeclared on a photographic style, just doing it my way all along, an accumulation of images emerged that embodies self-reflection. Here are those photos.

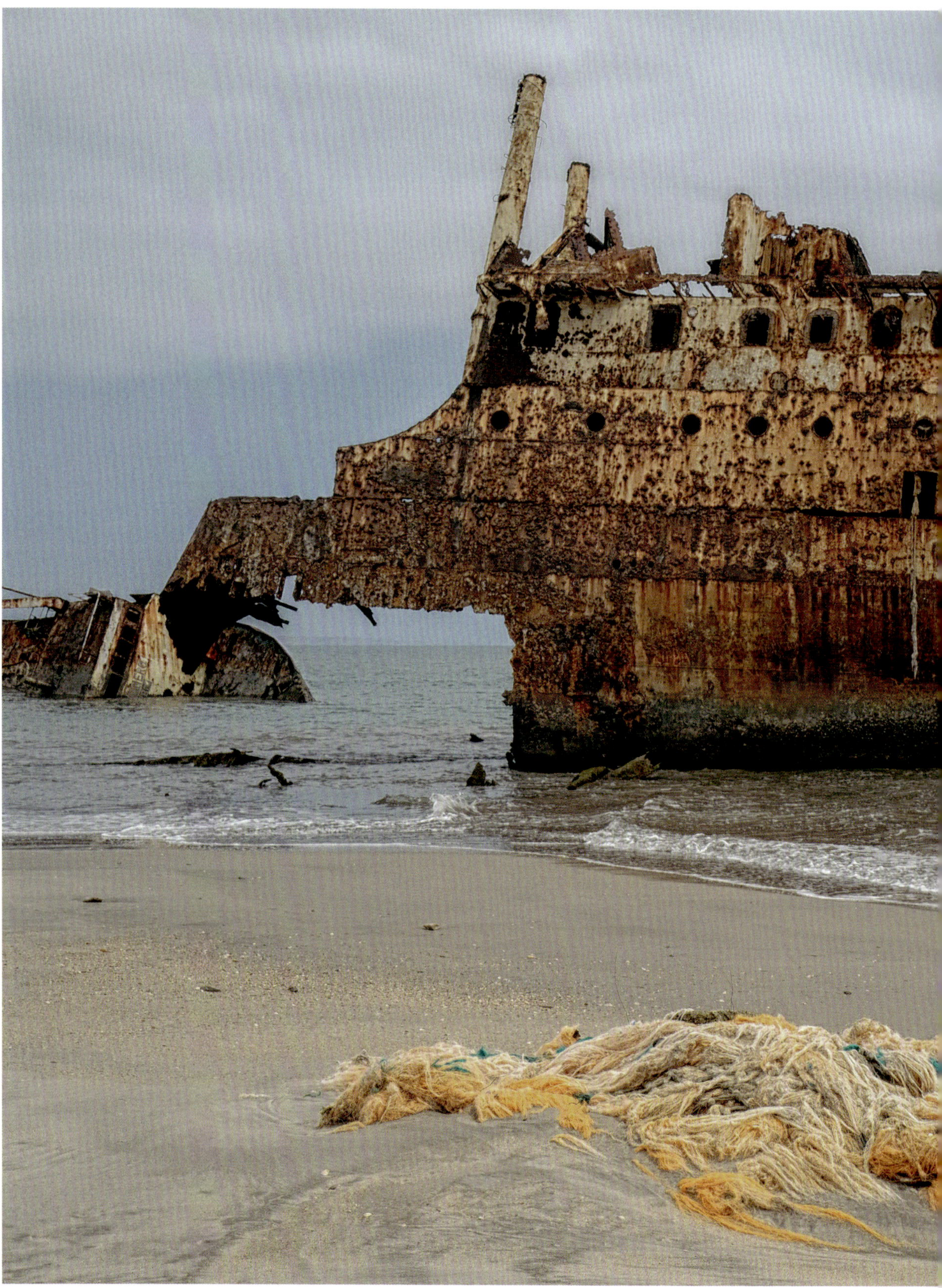

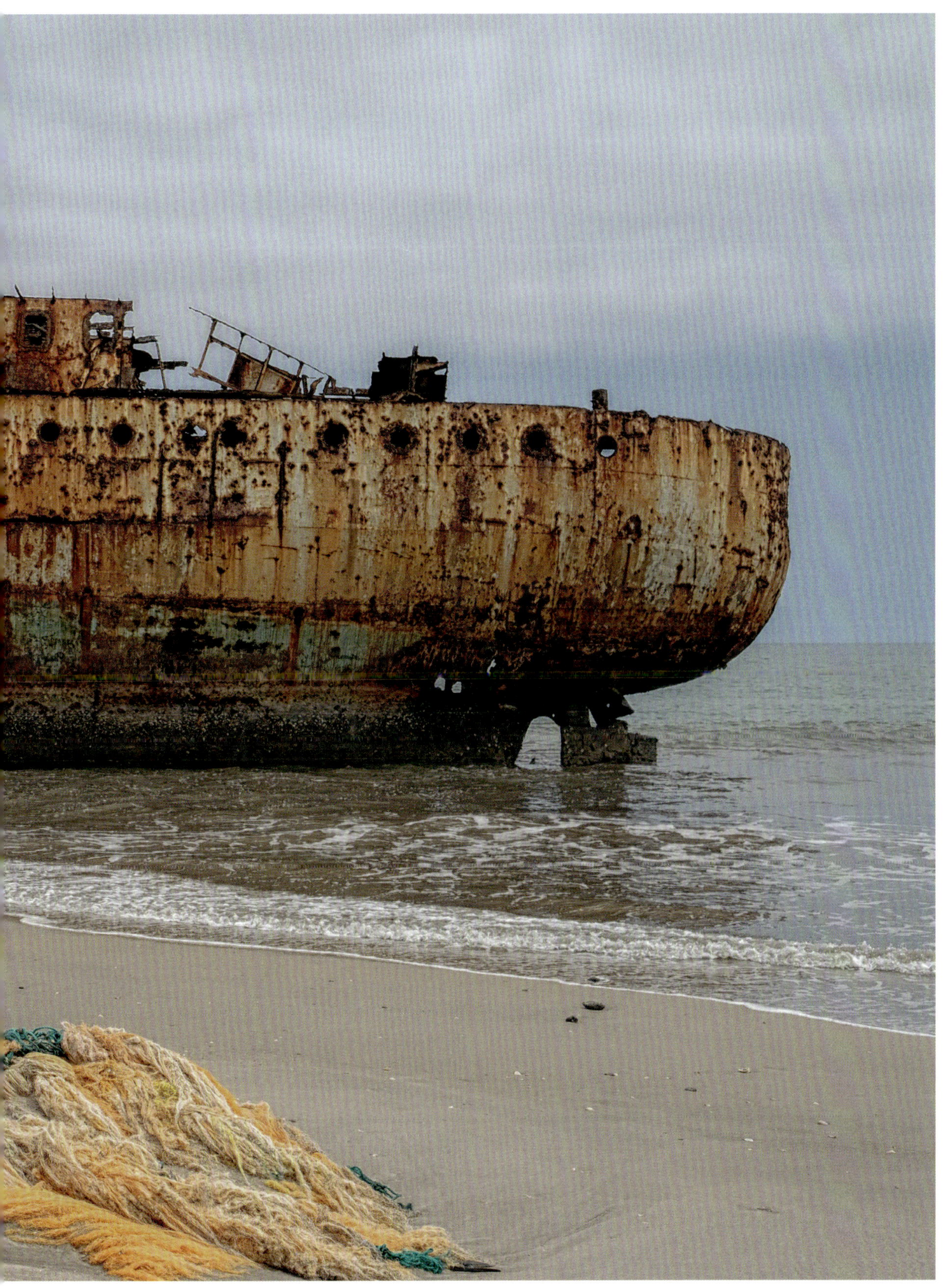

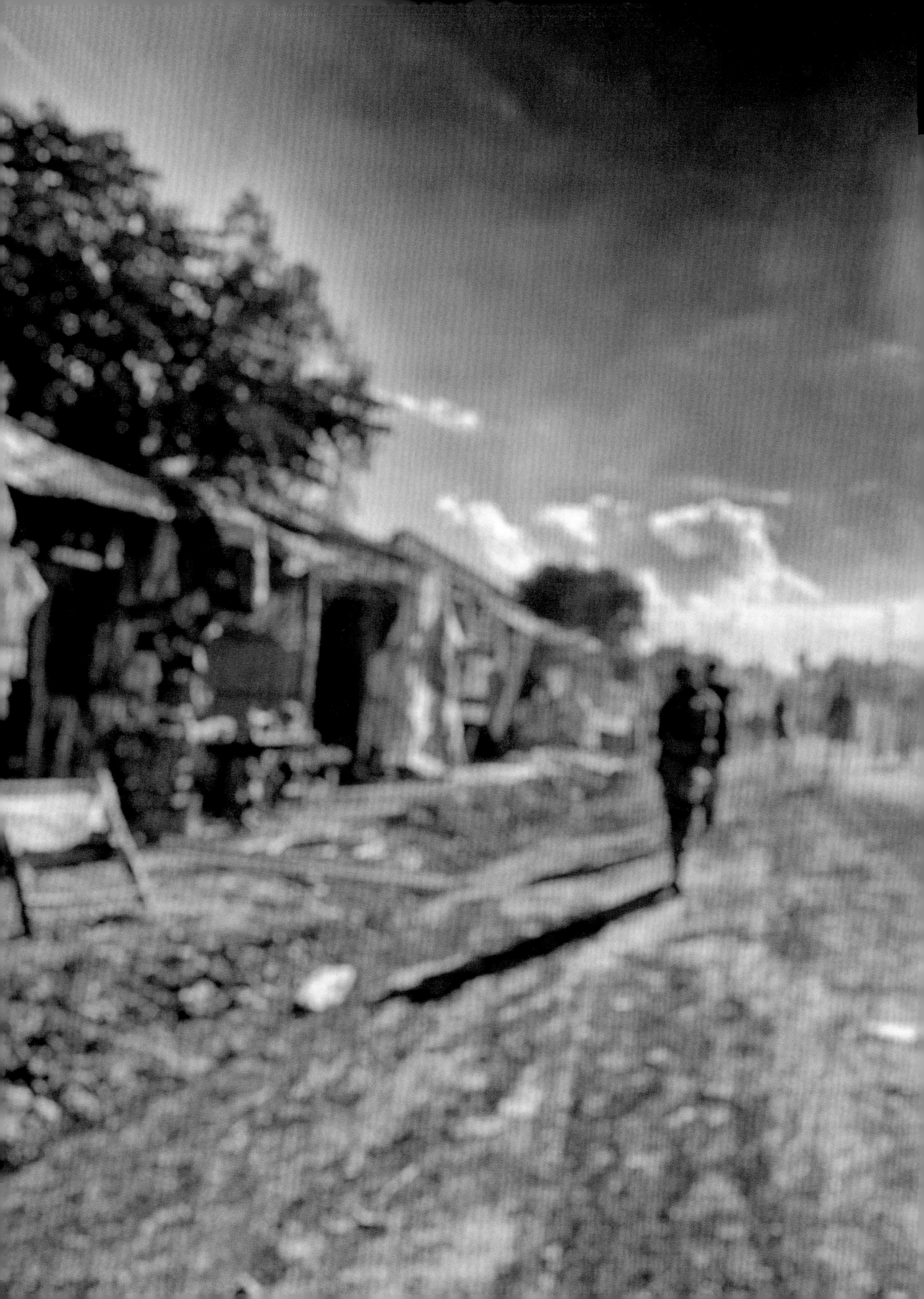

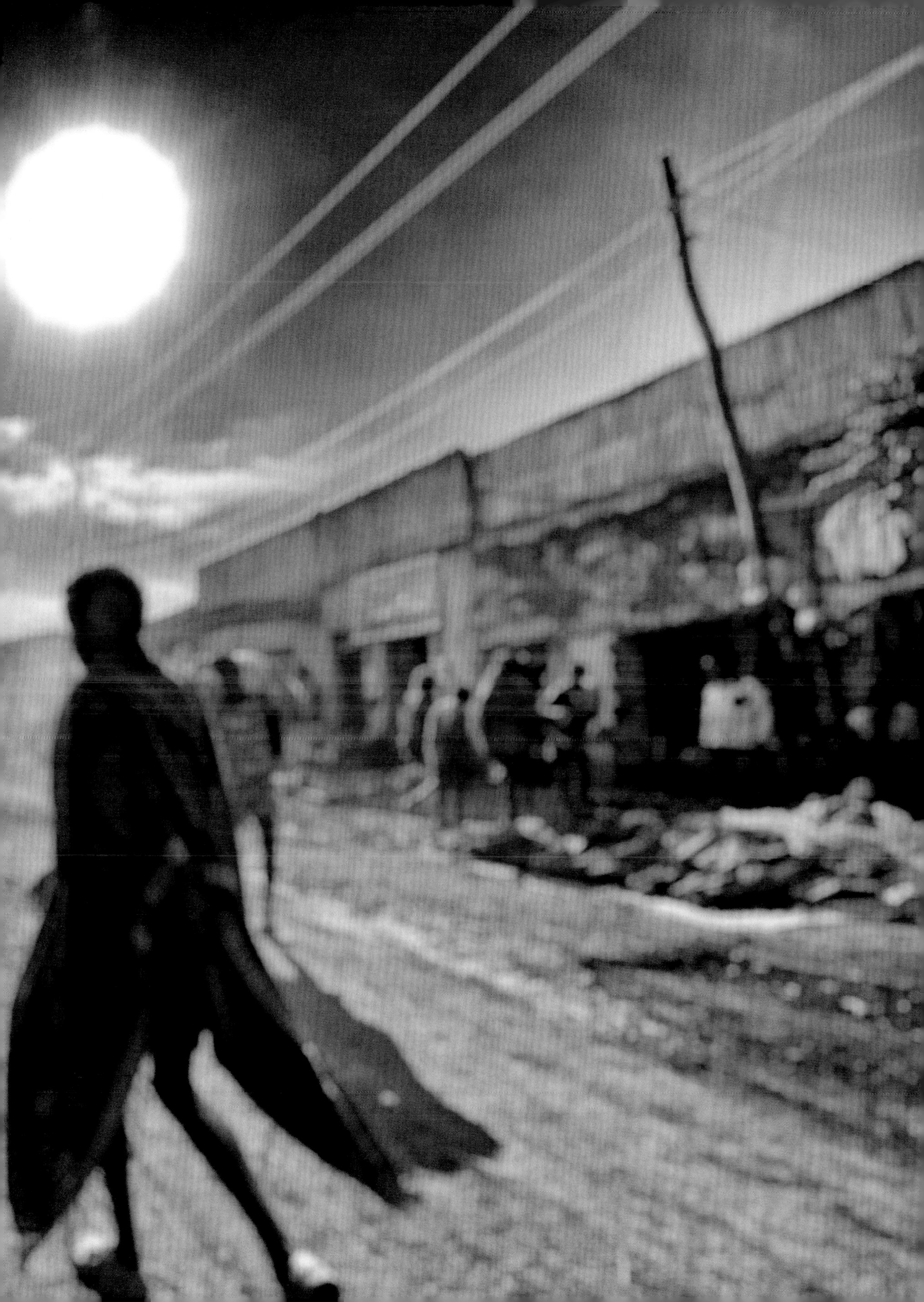

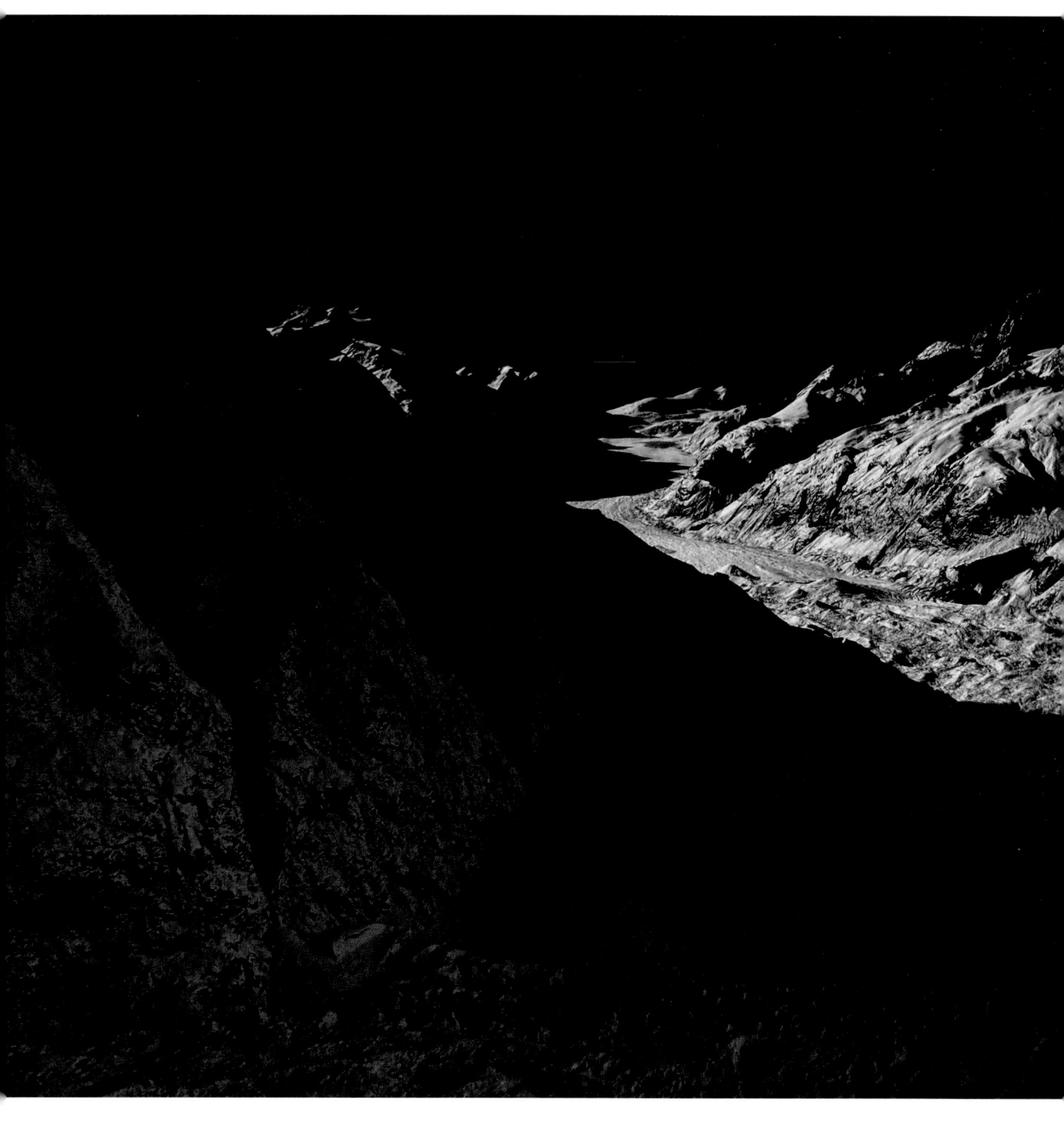

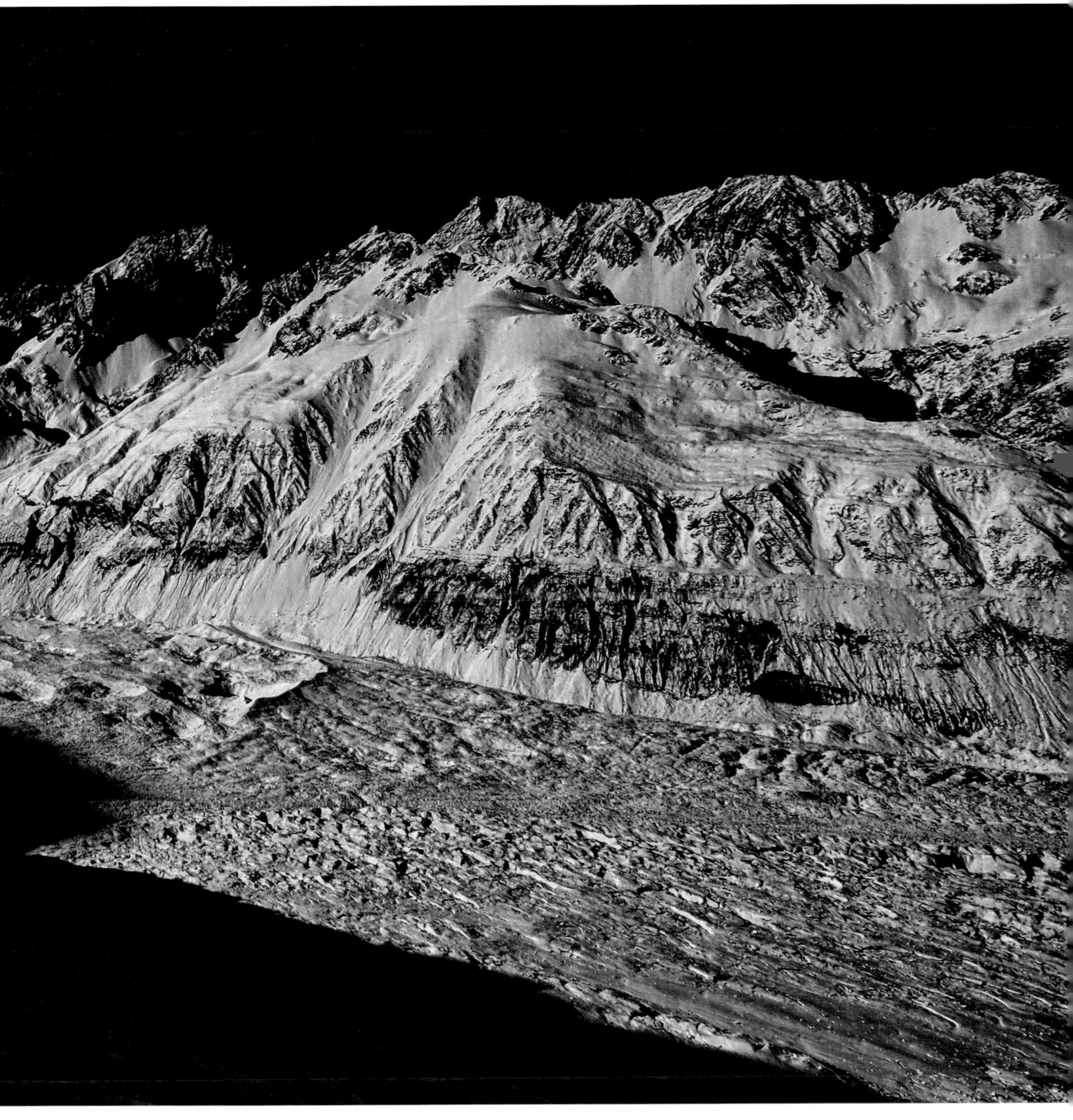

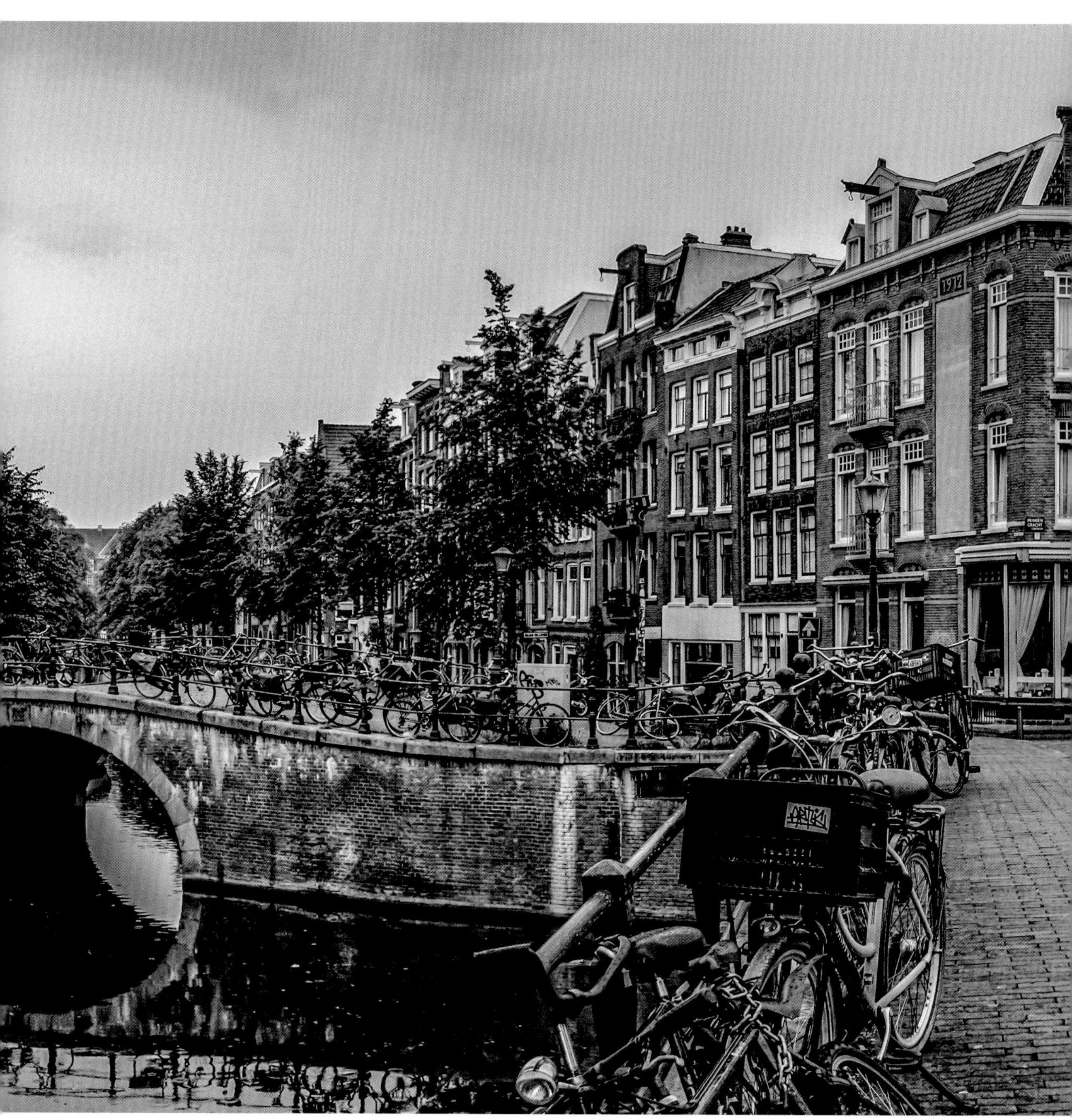

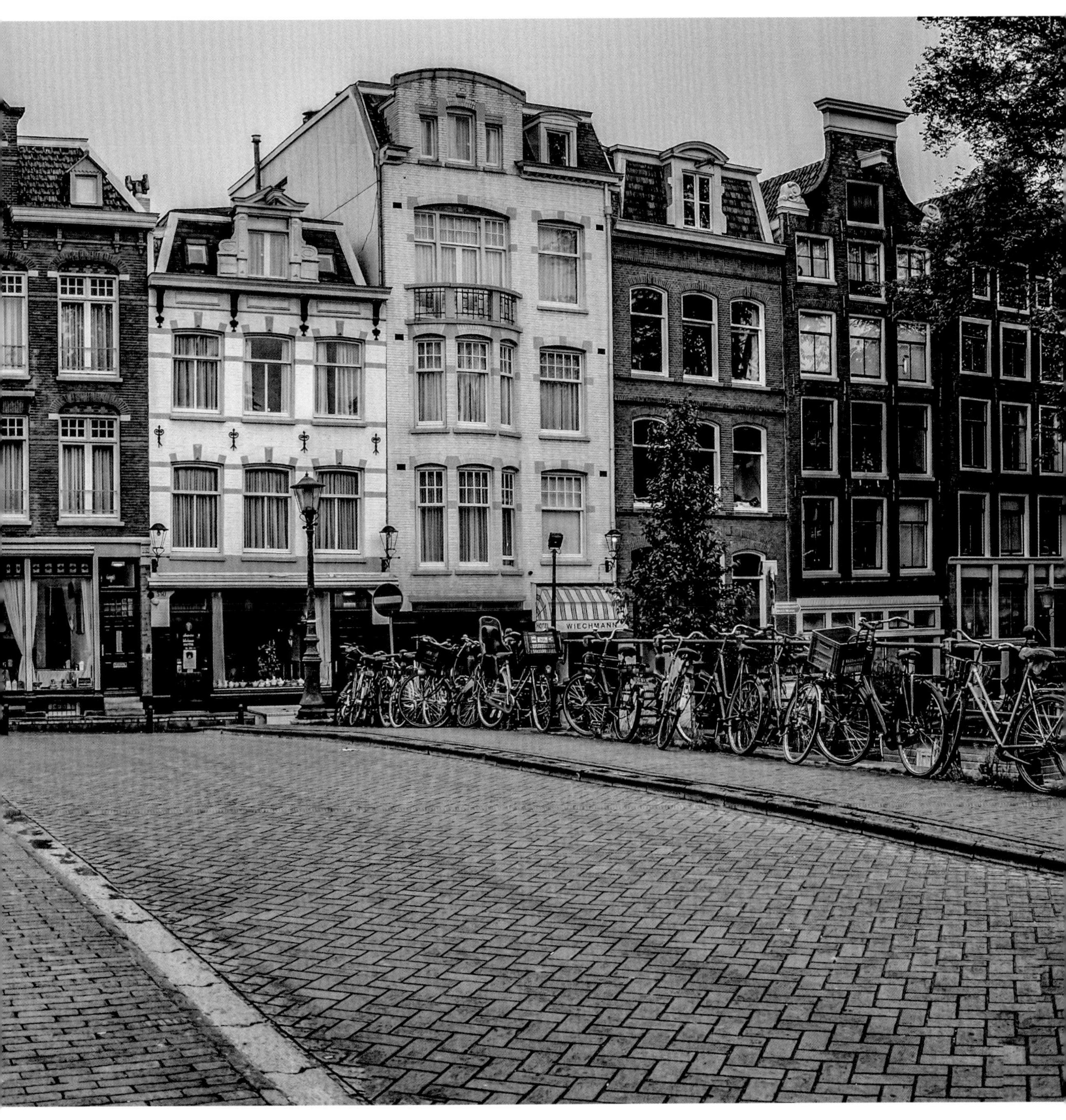

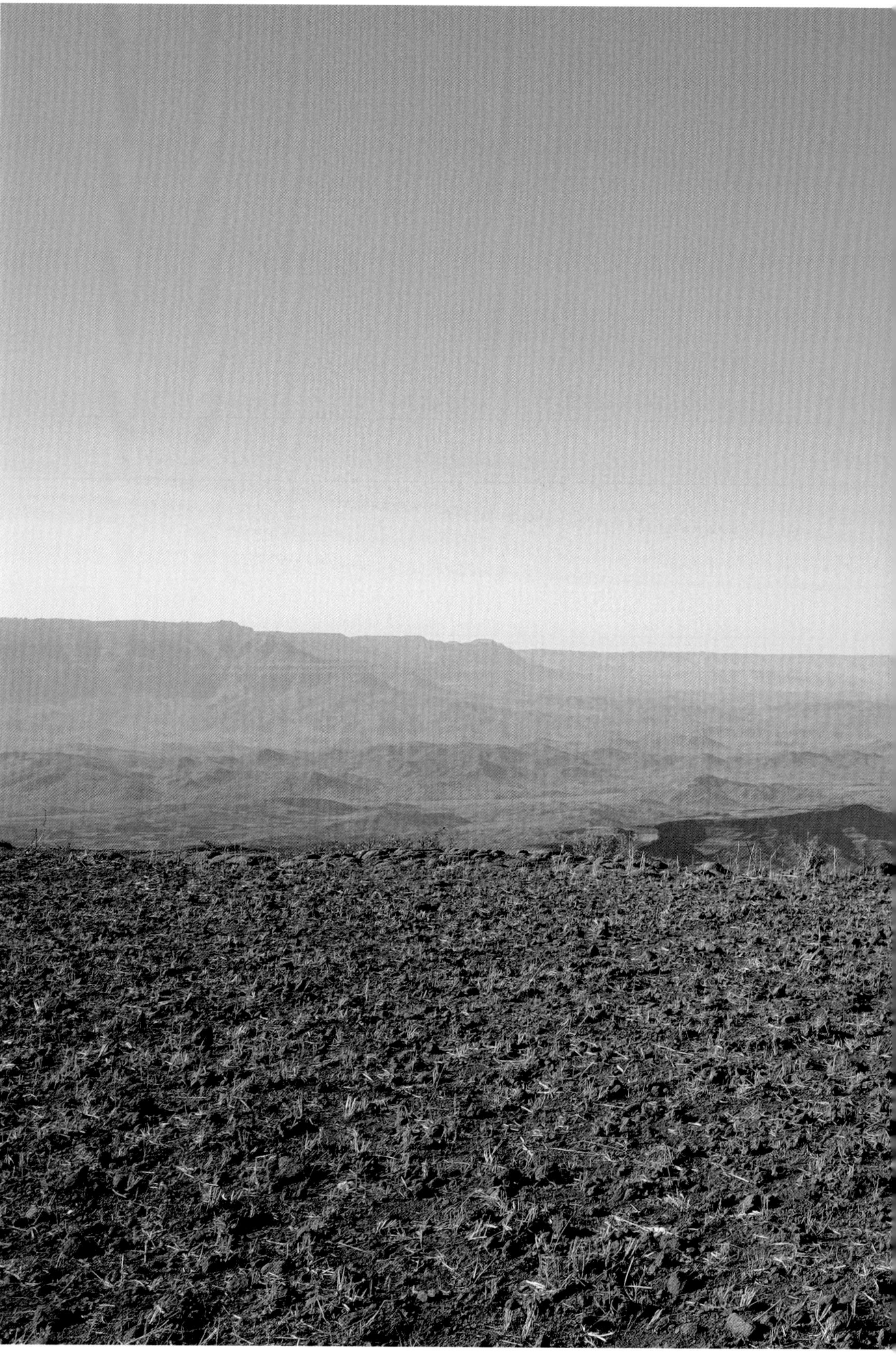

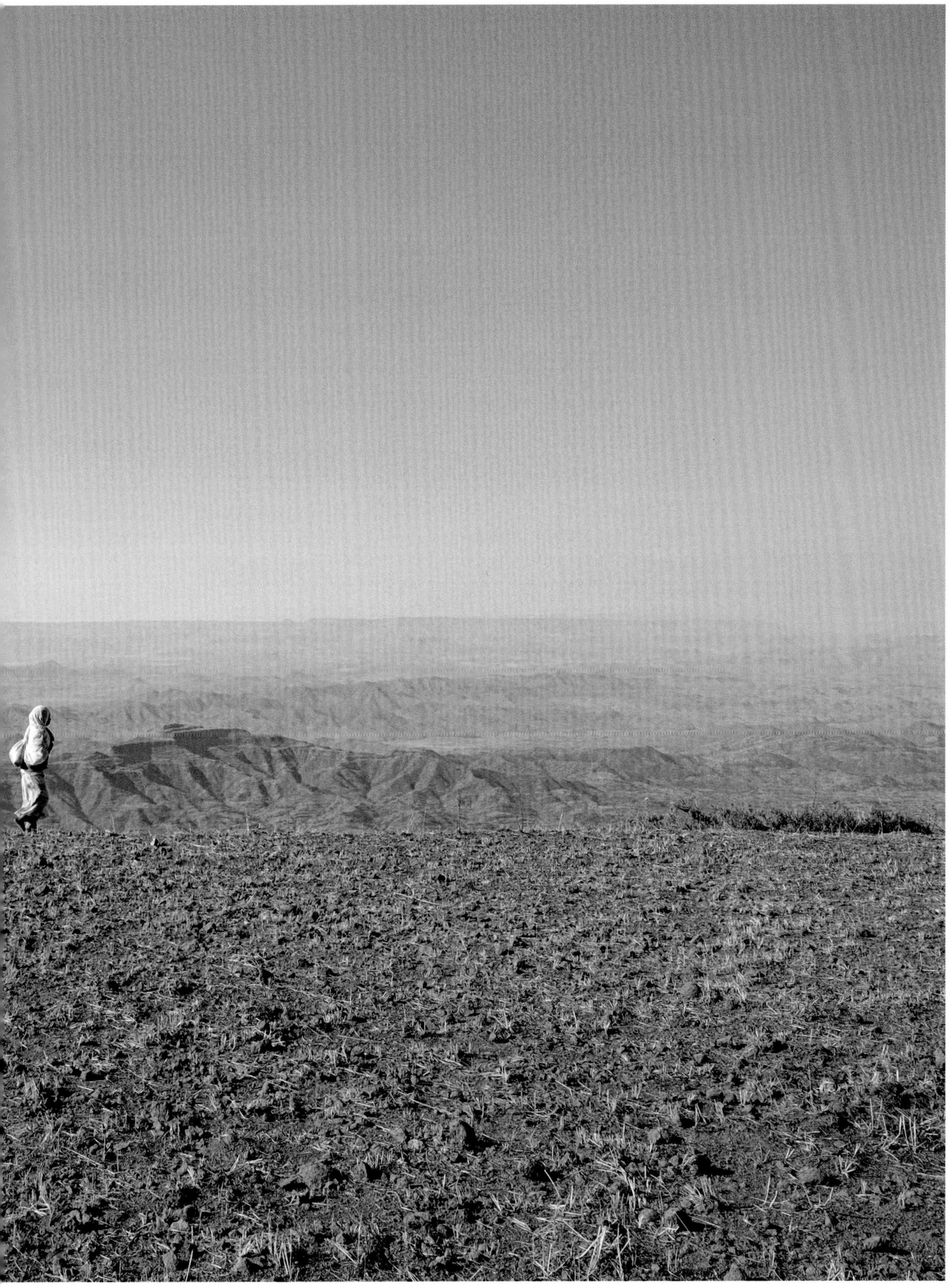

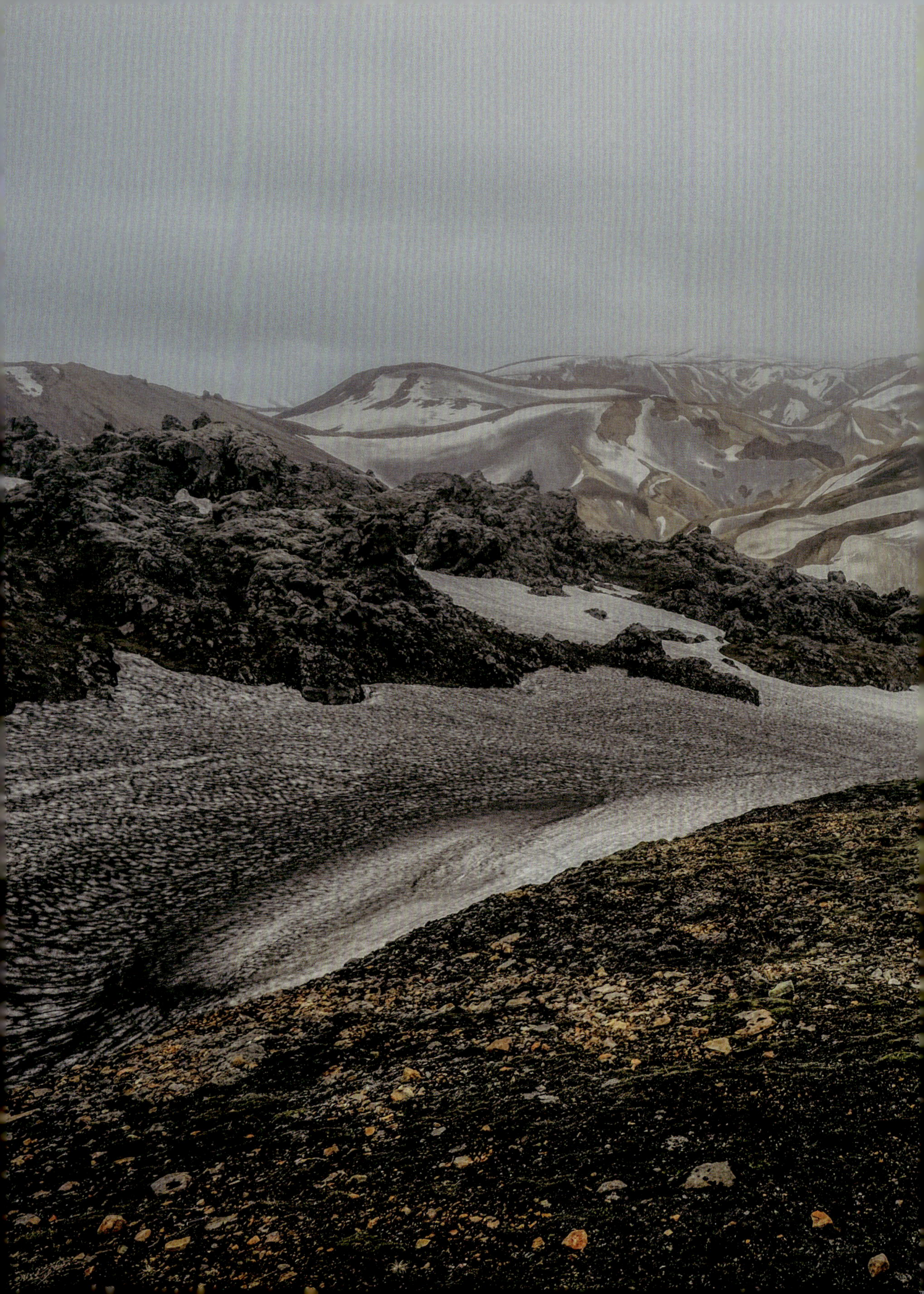

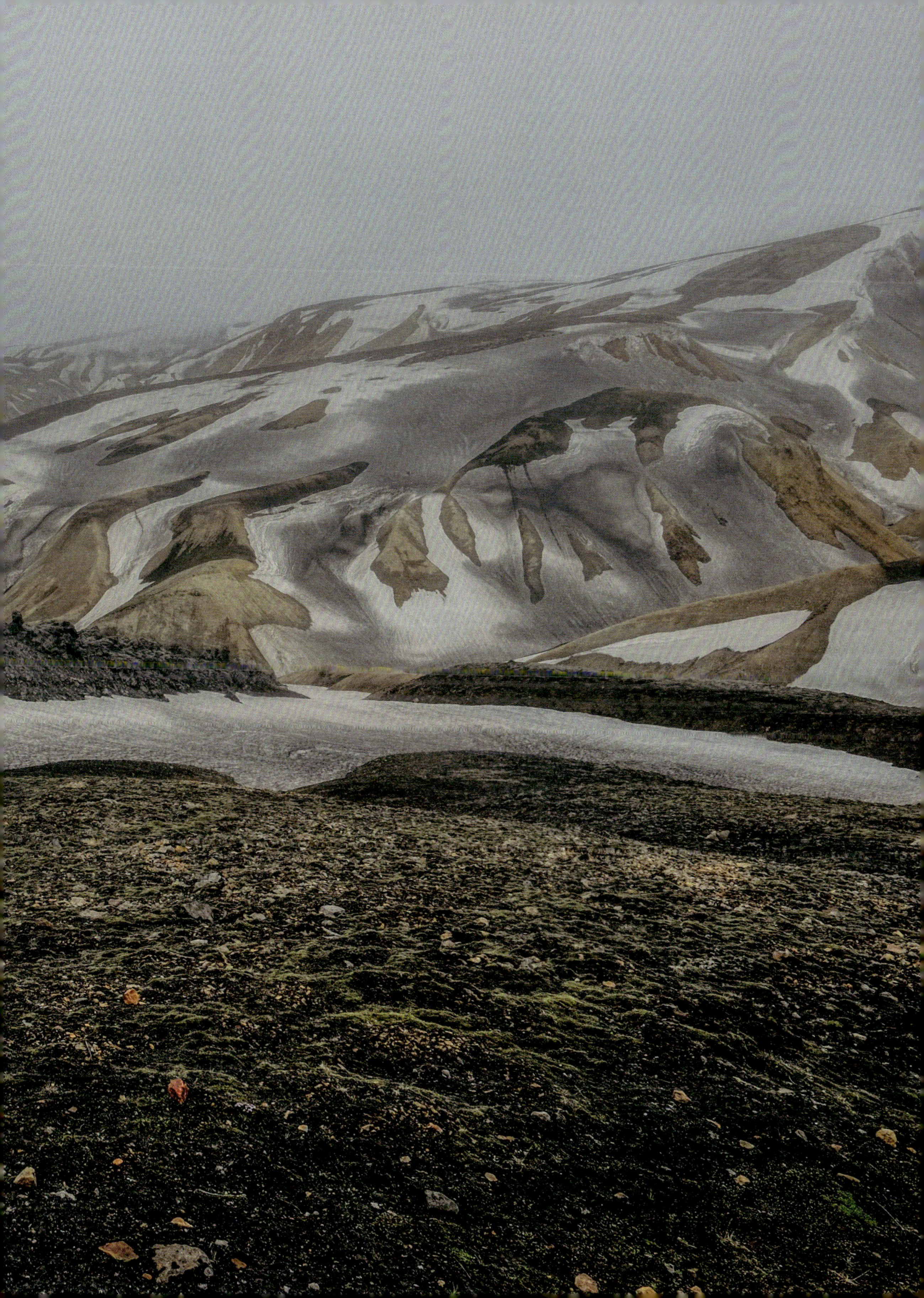

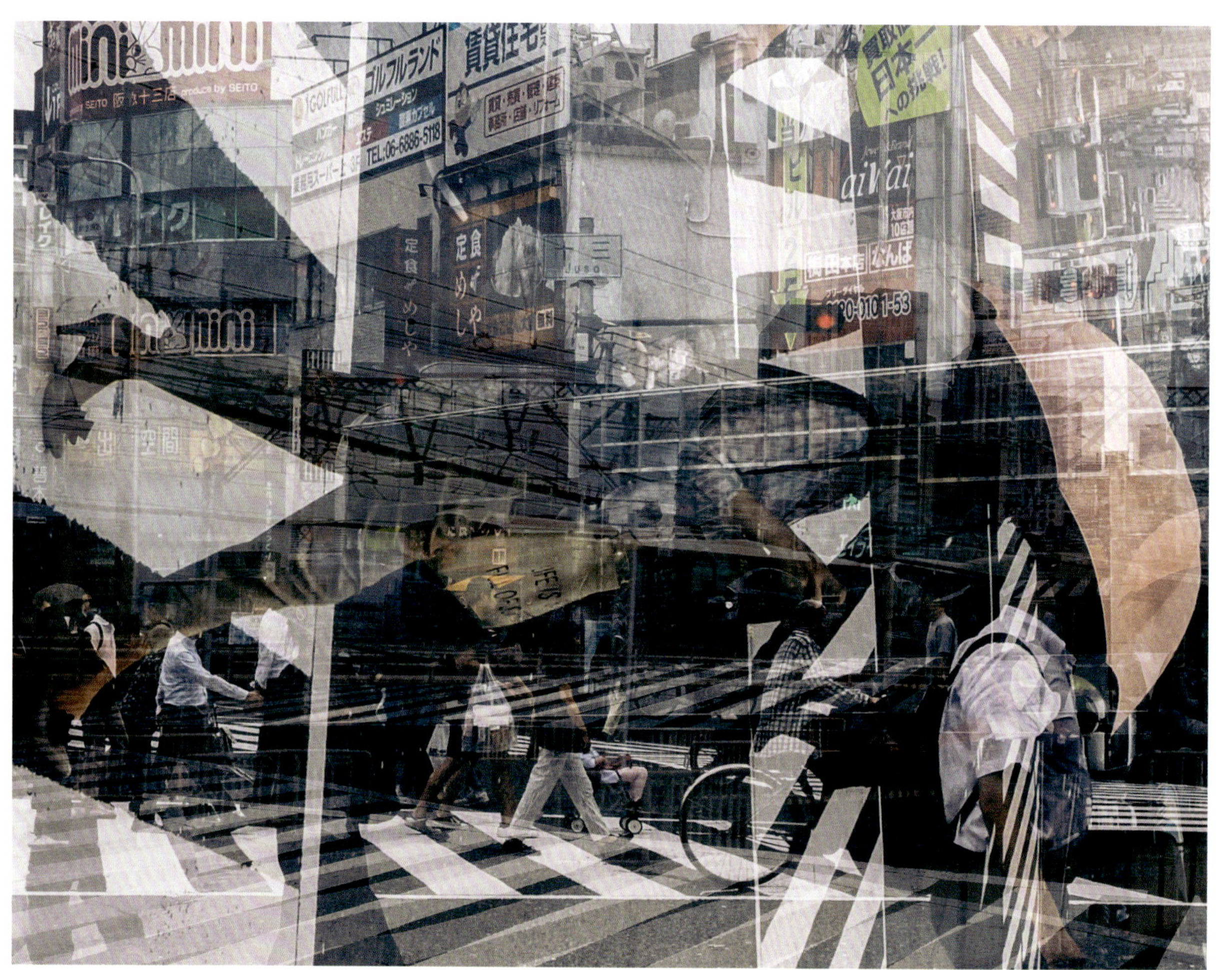

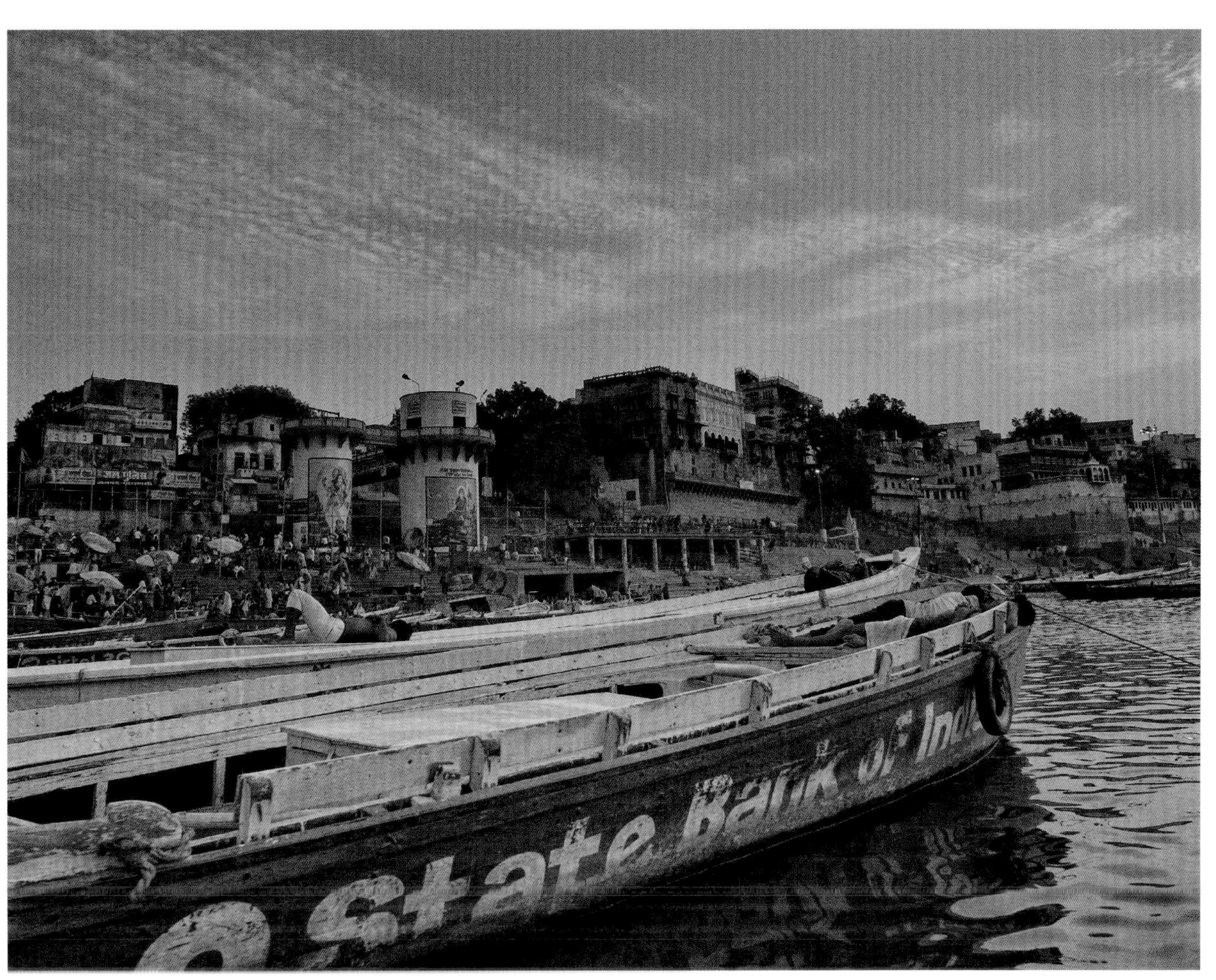

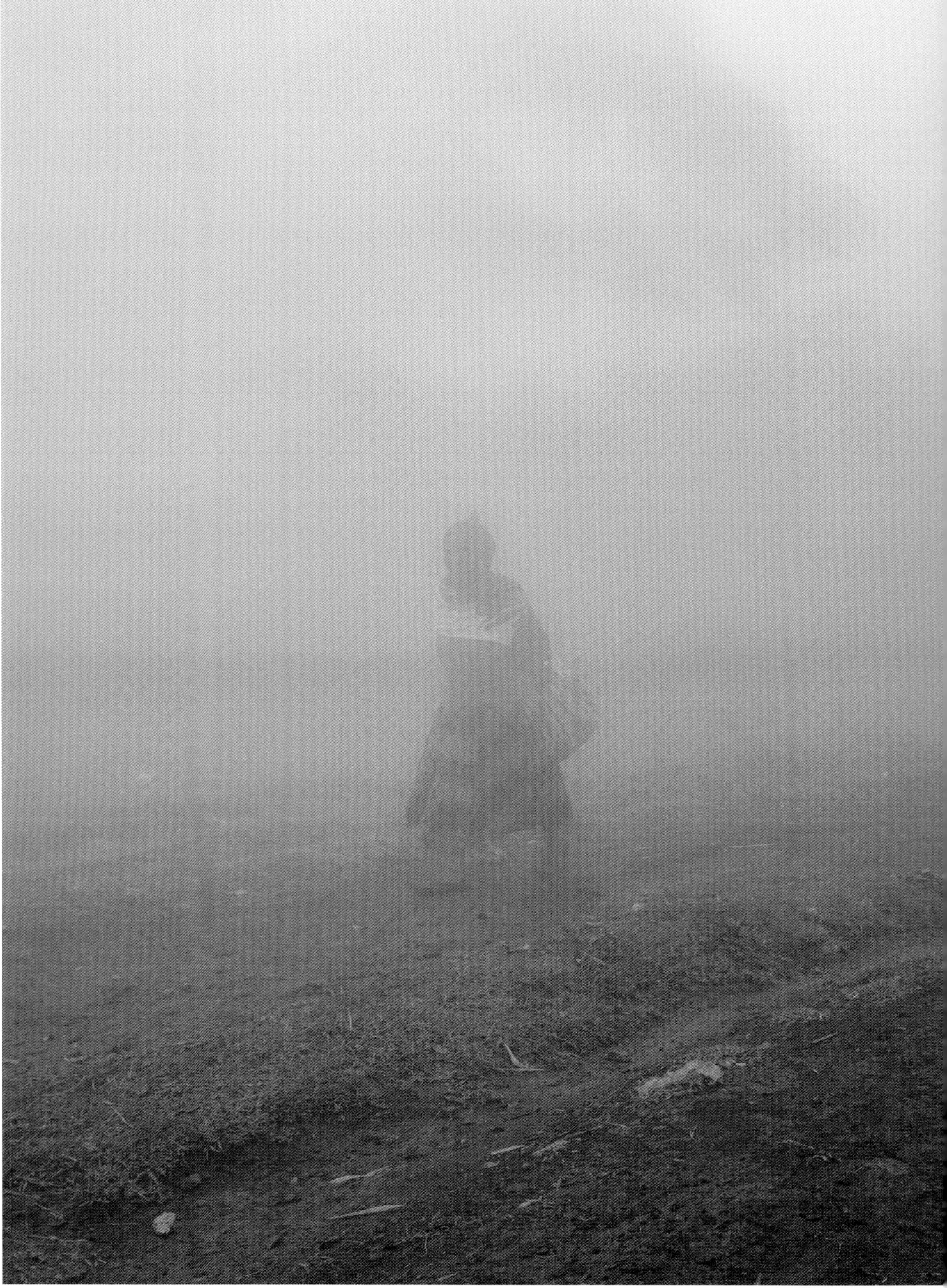

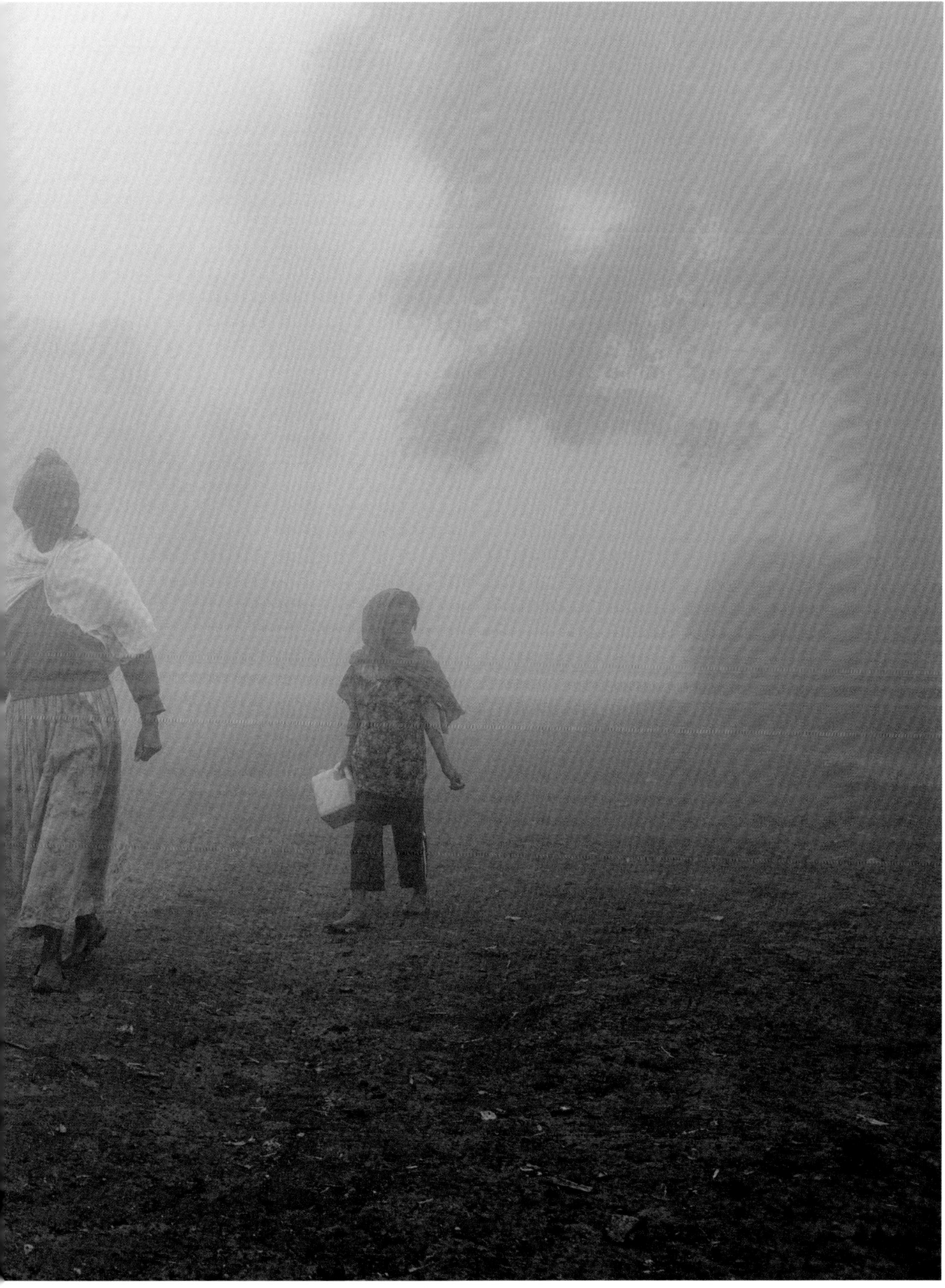

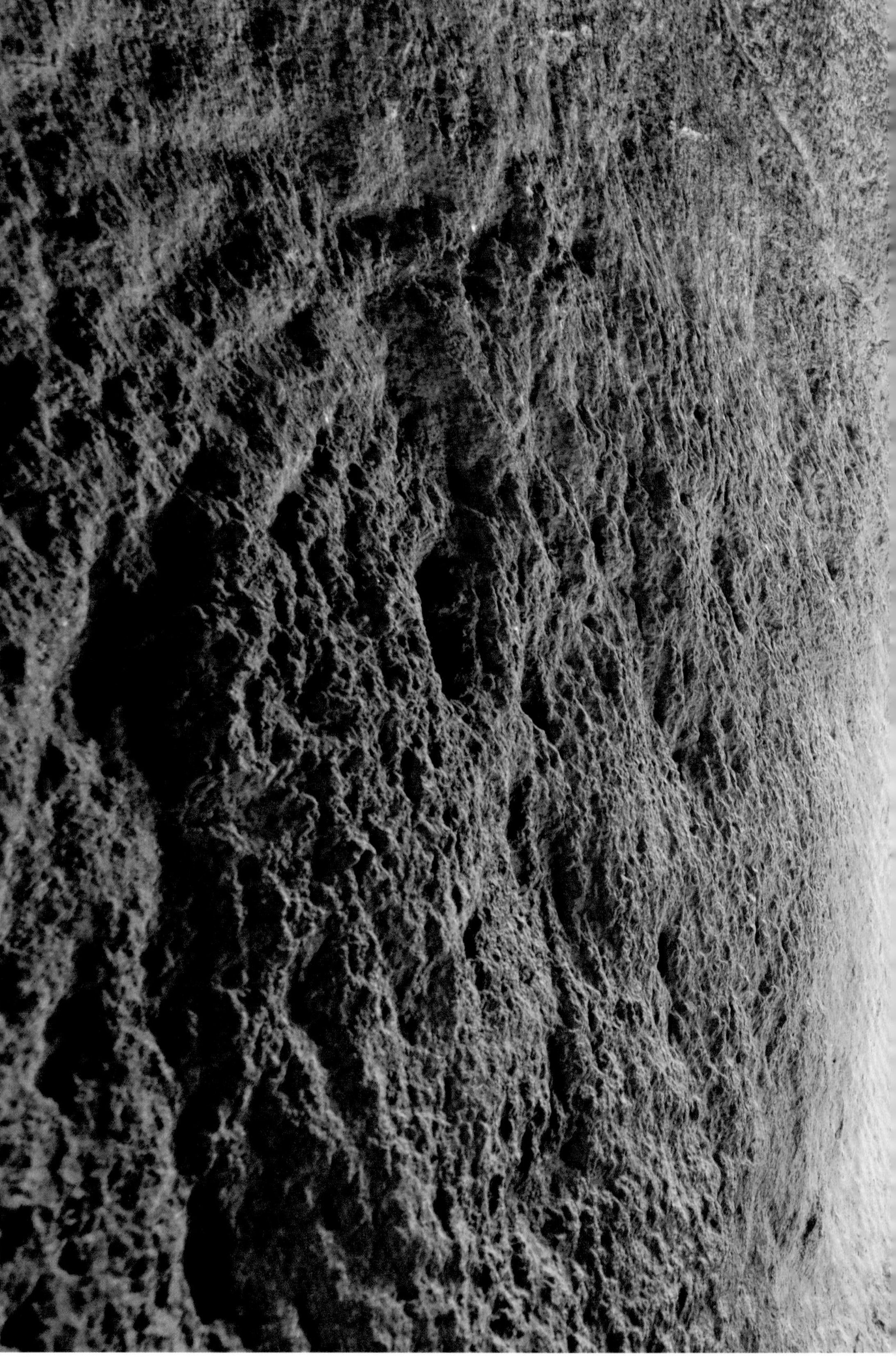

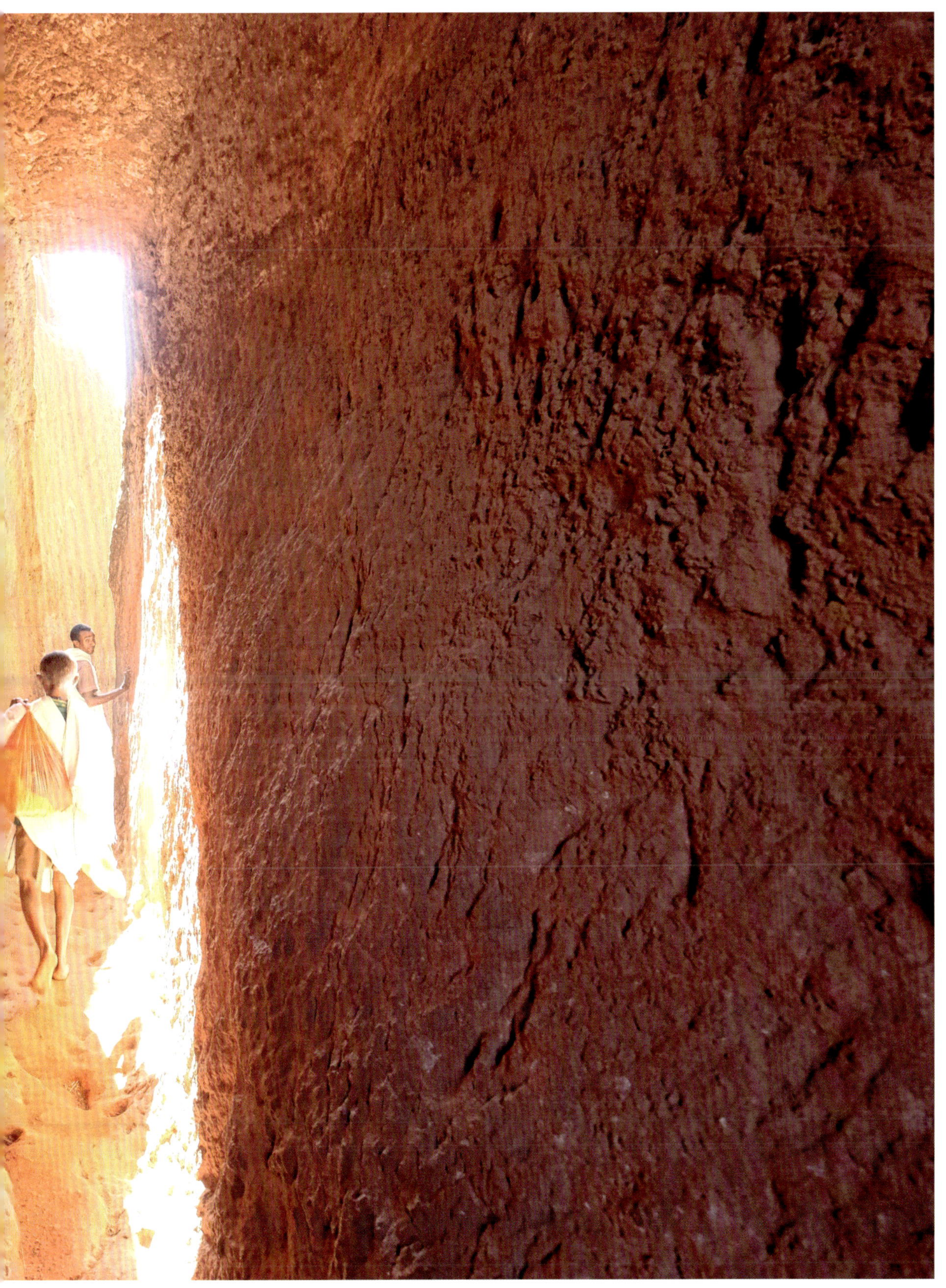

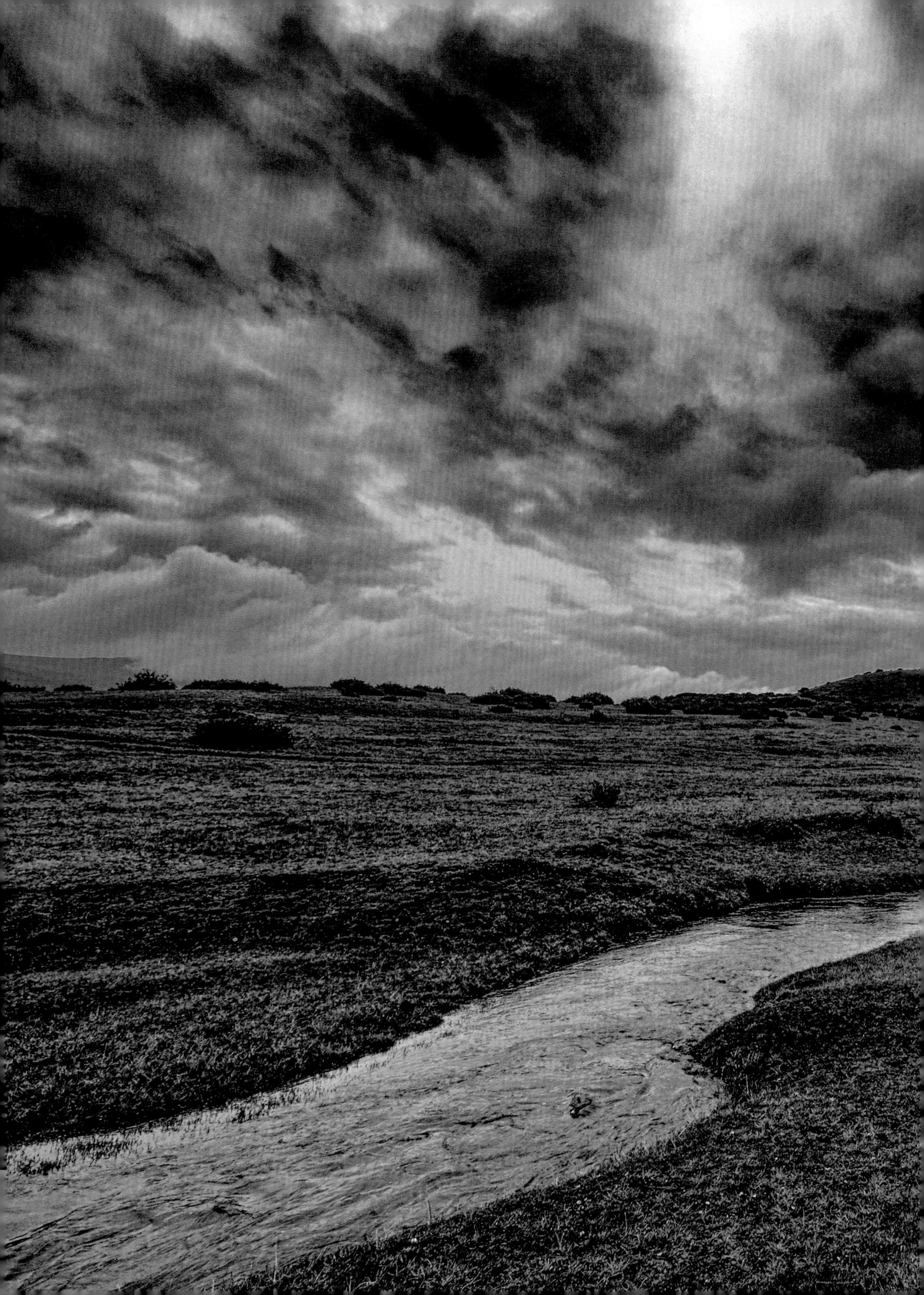

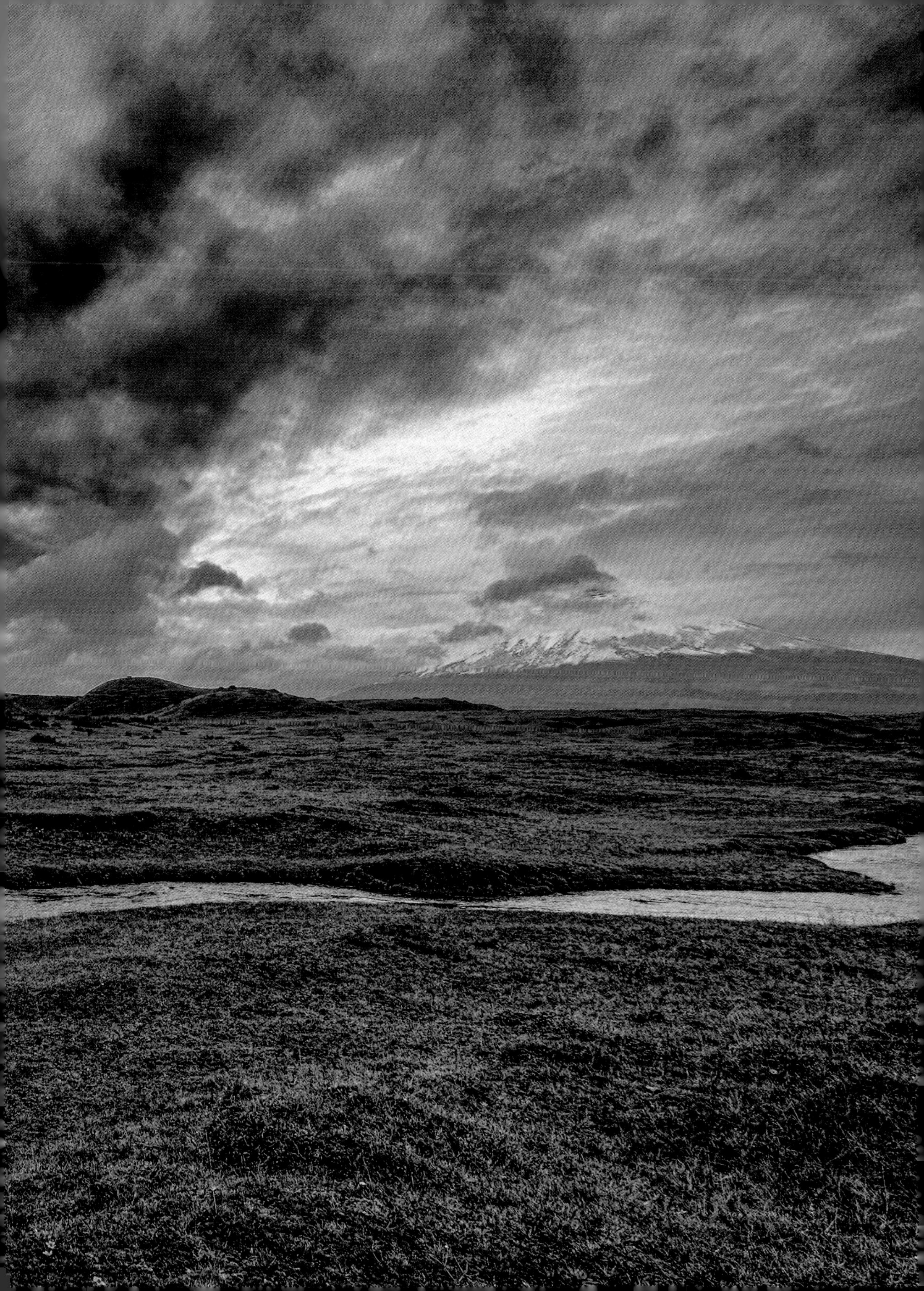

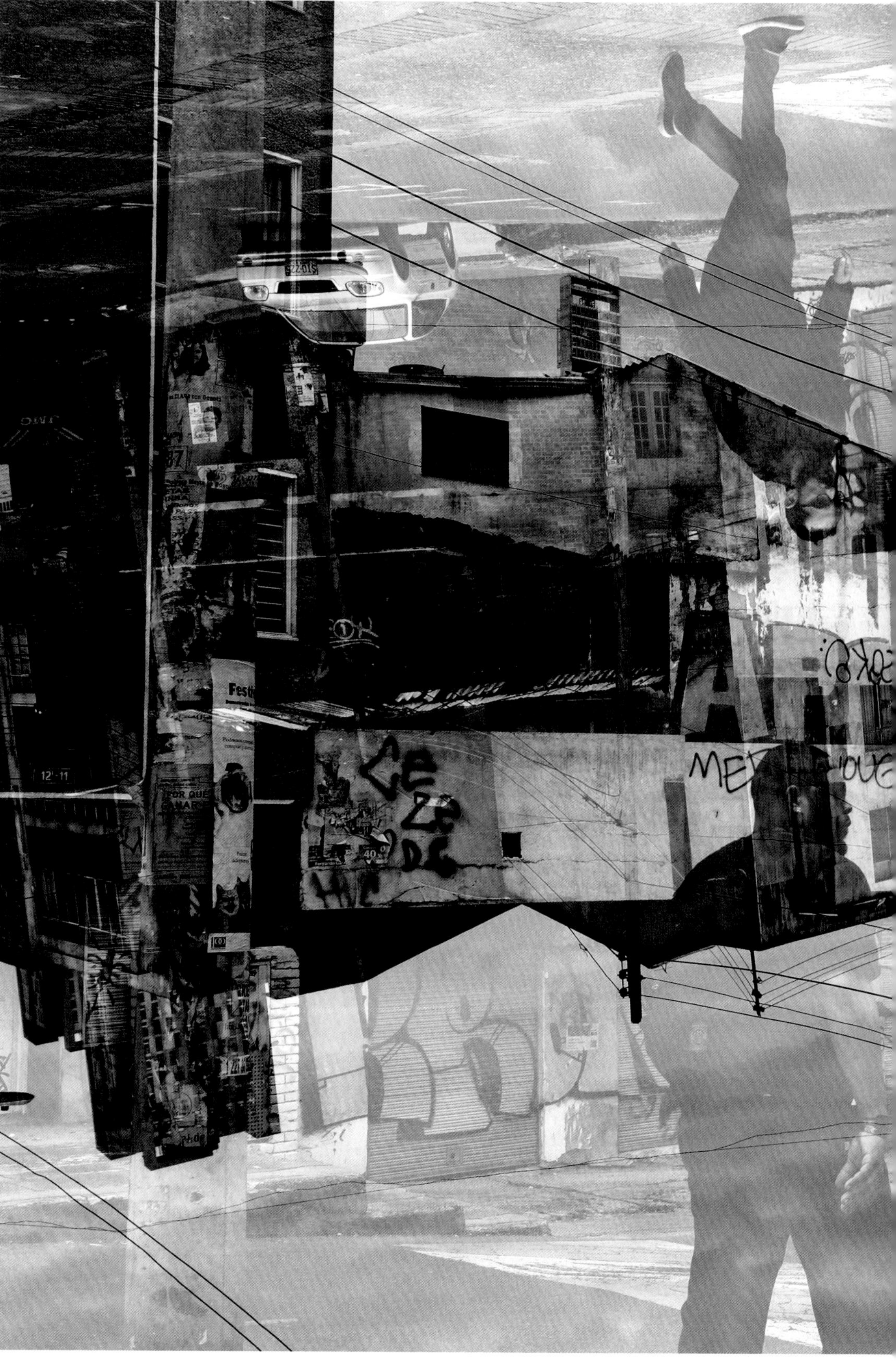

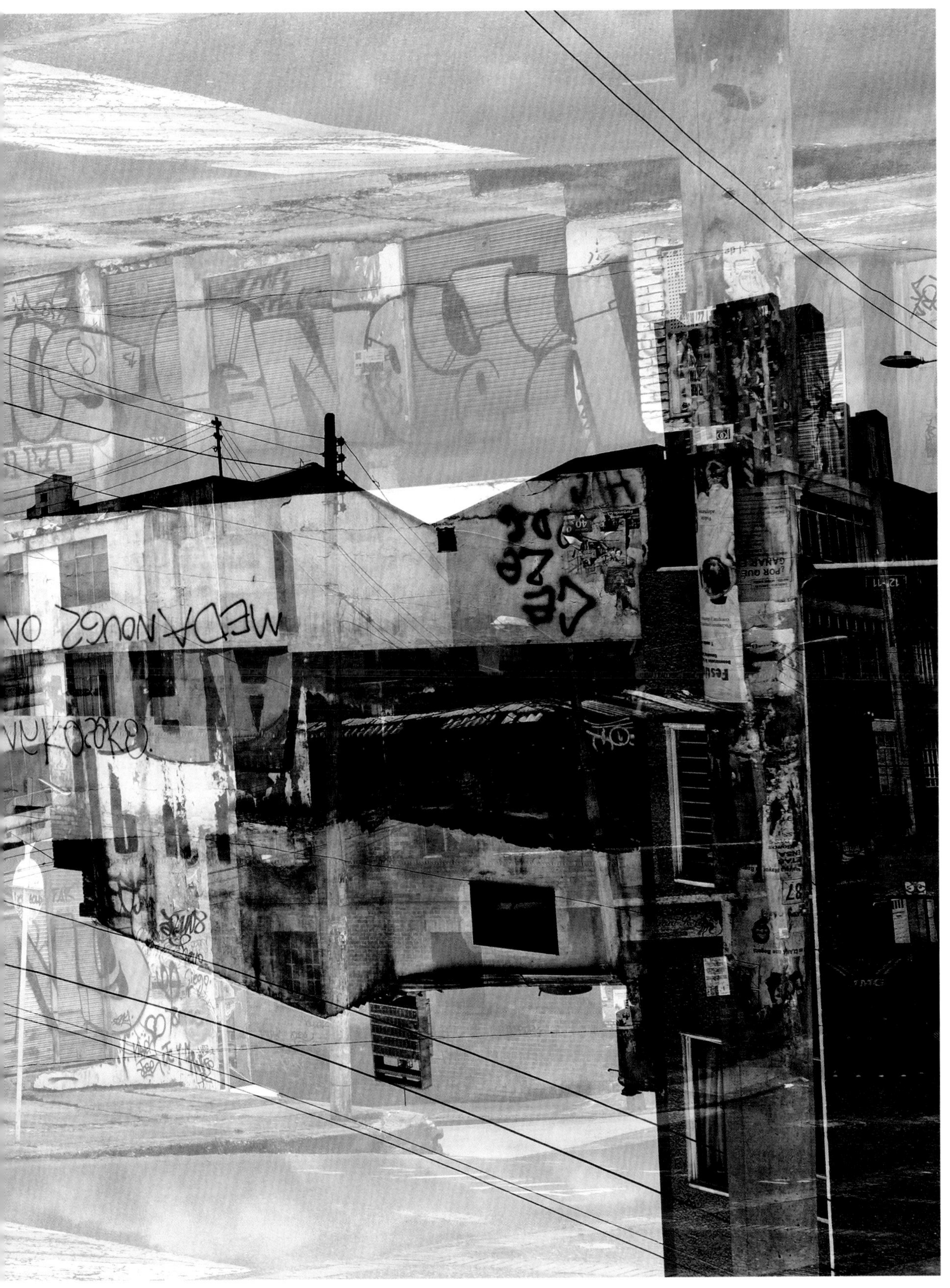

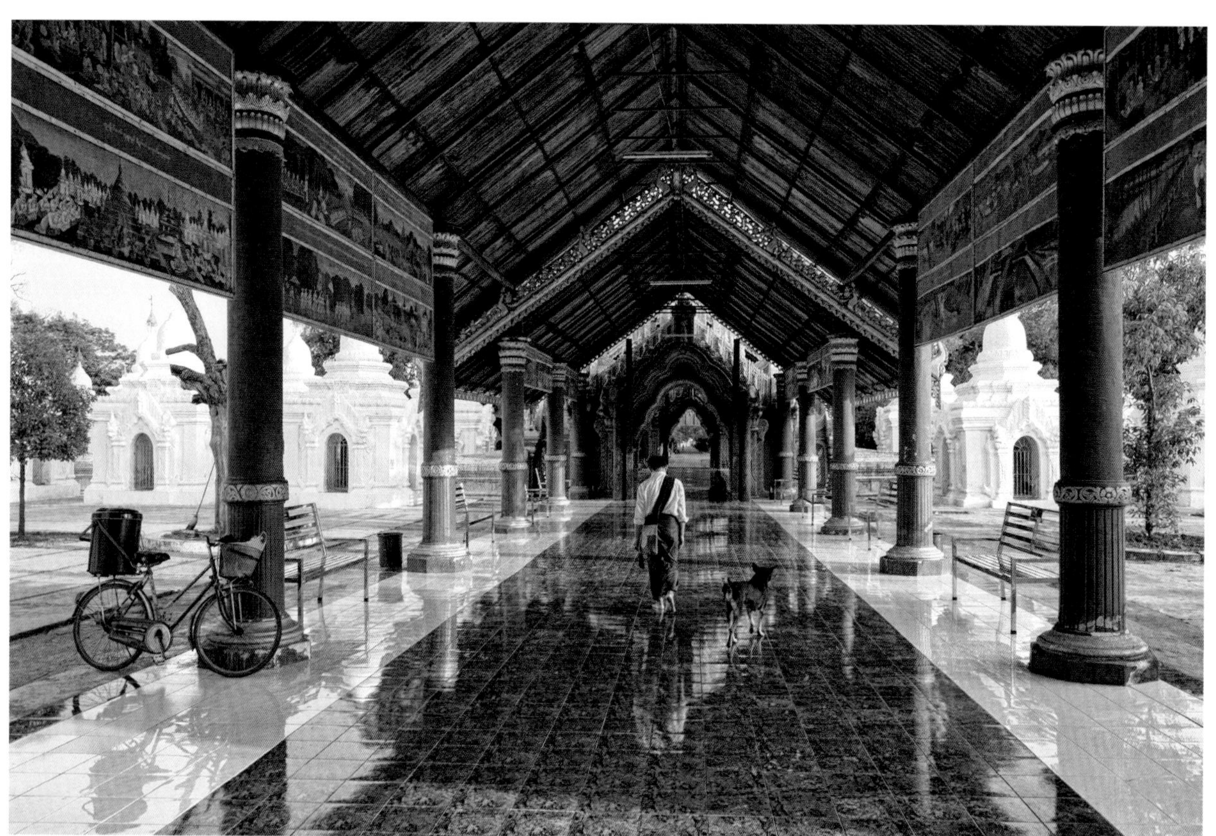

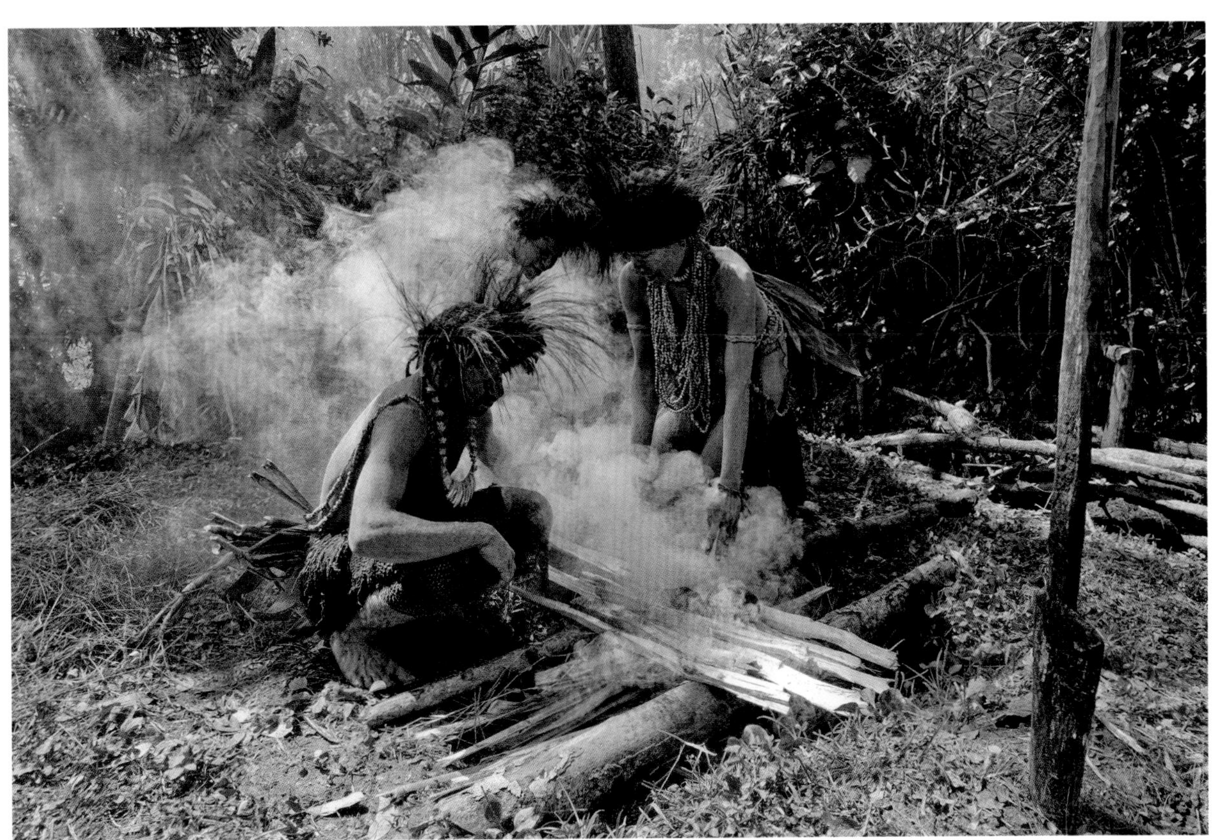

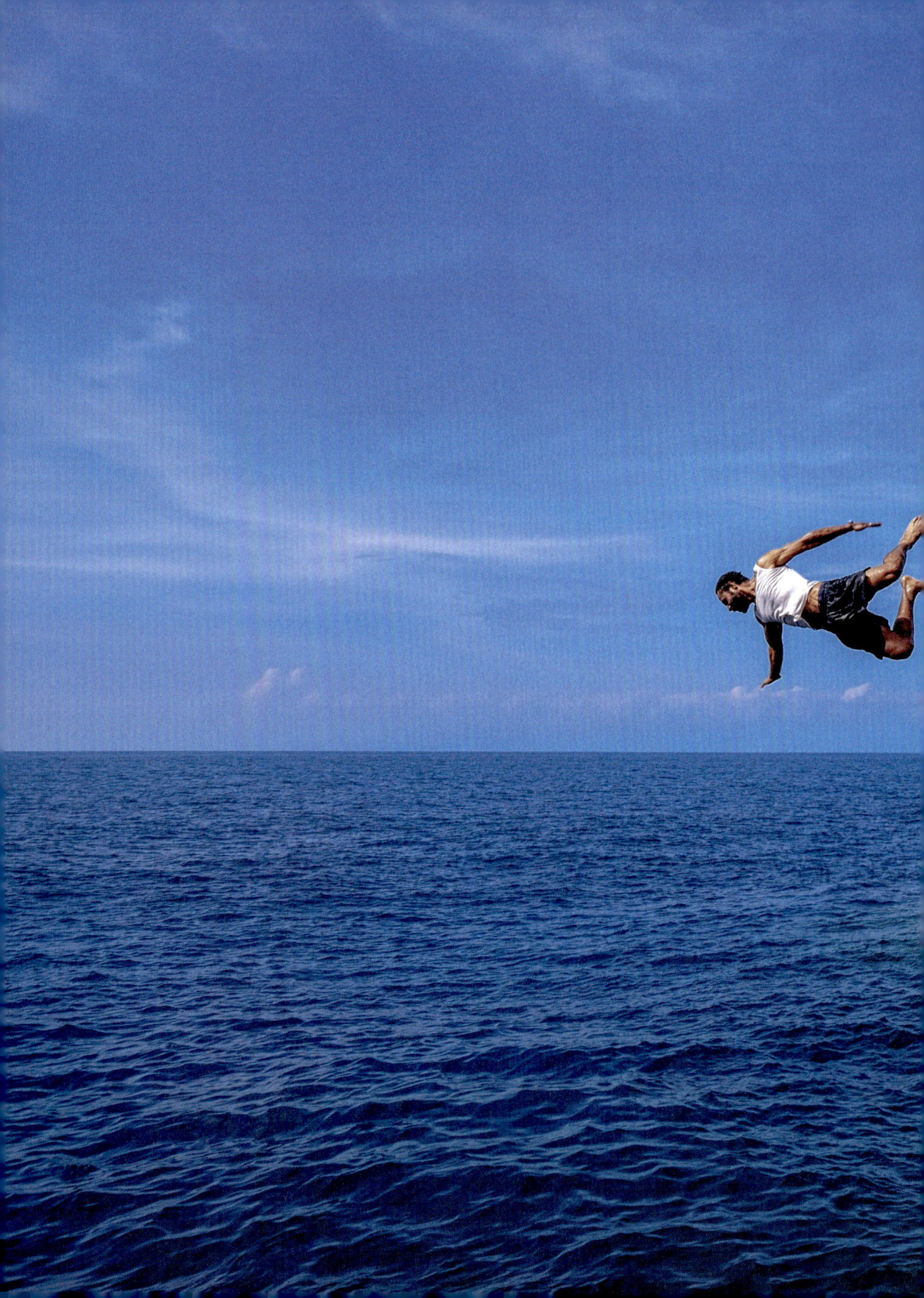

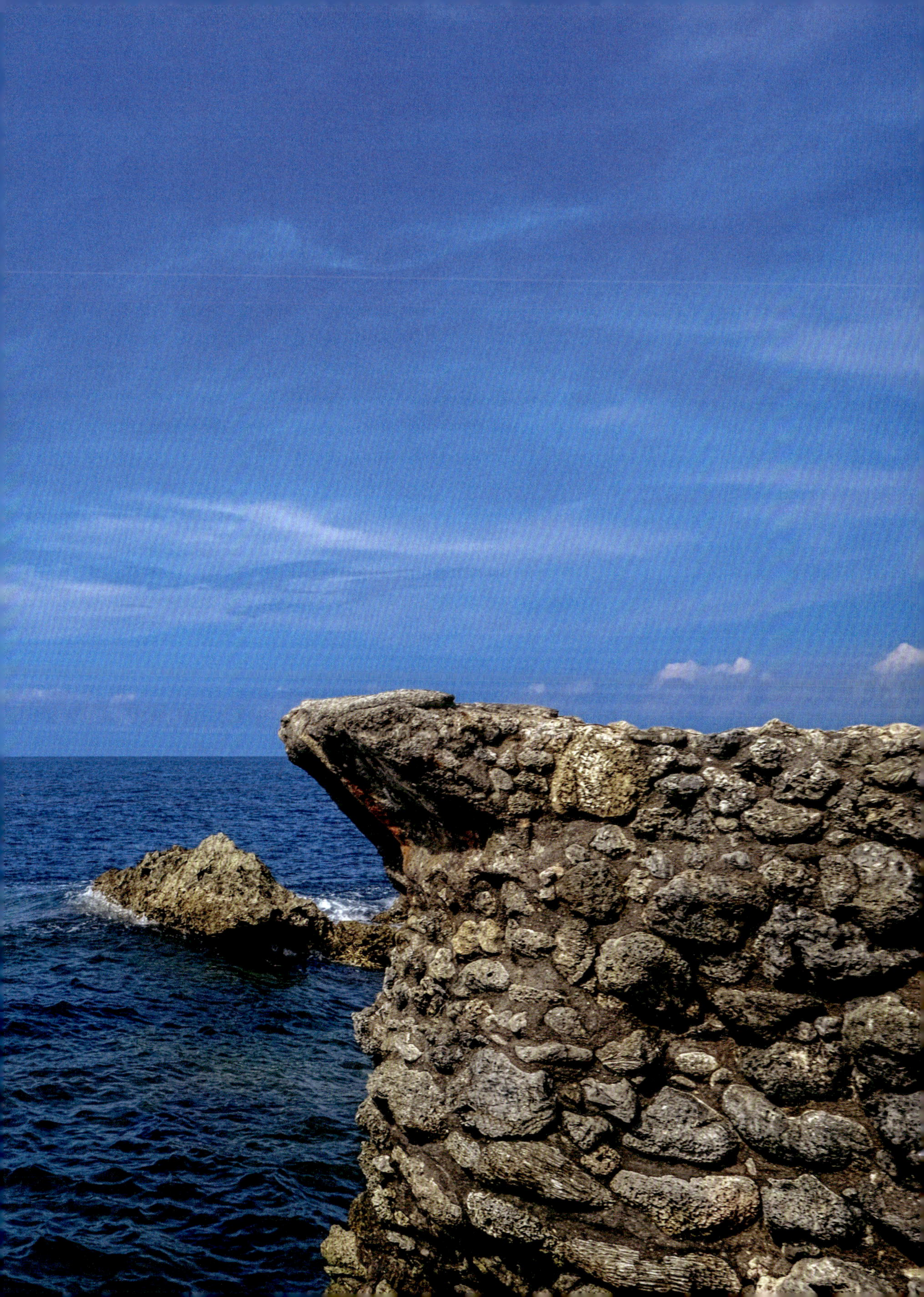

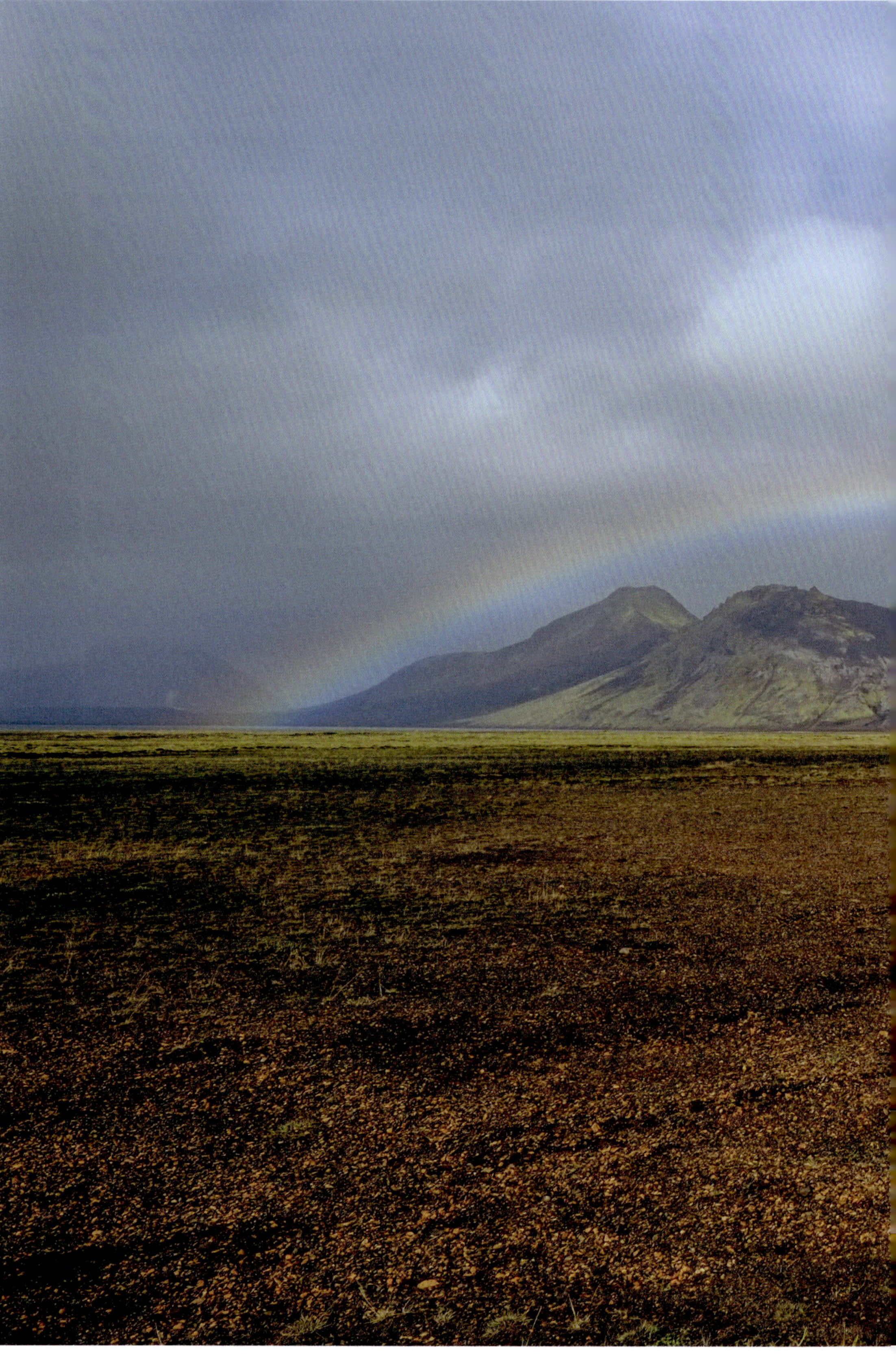

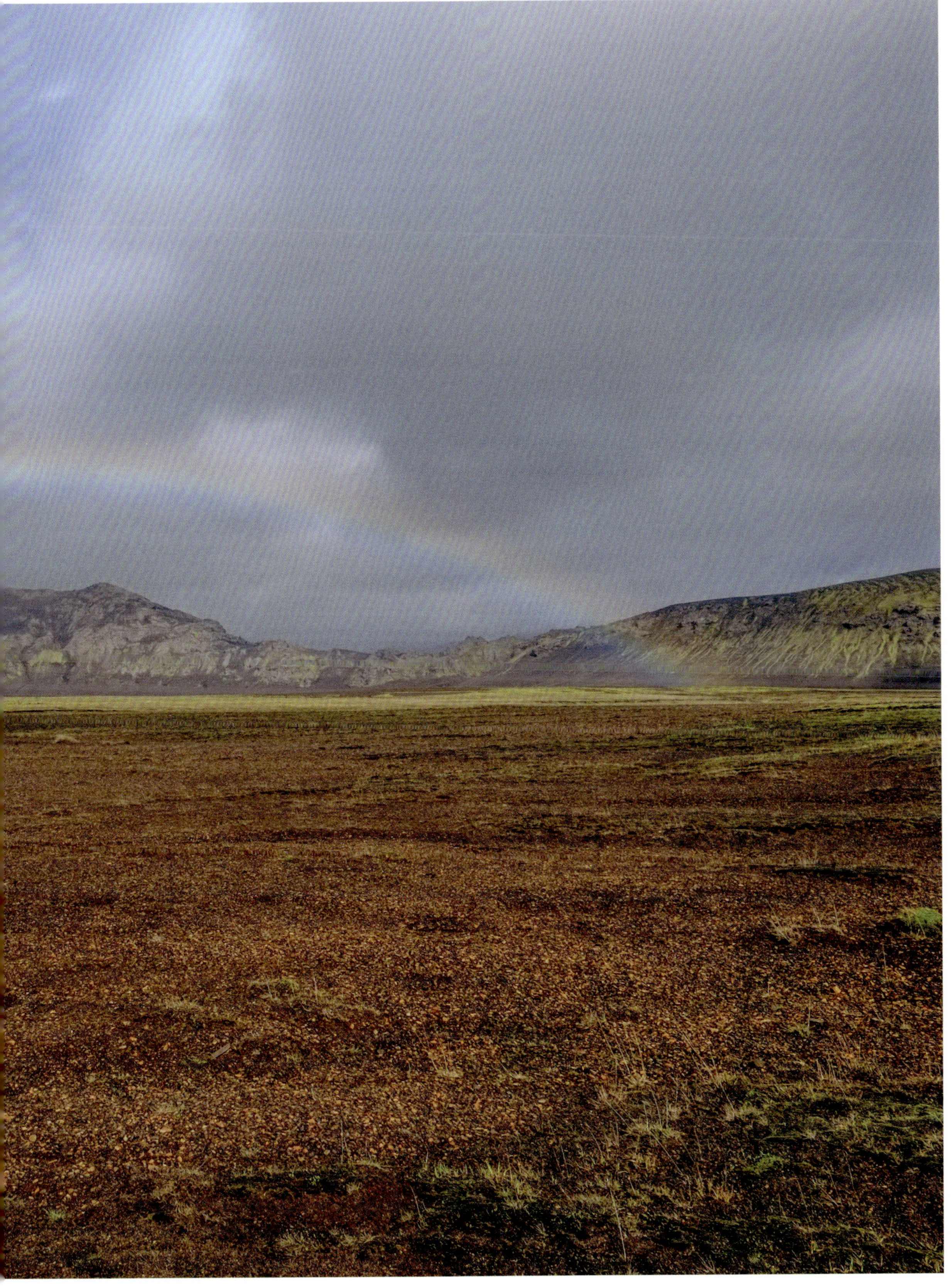

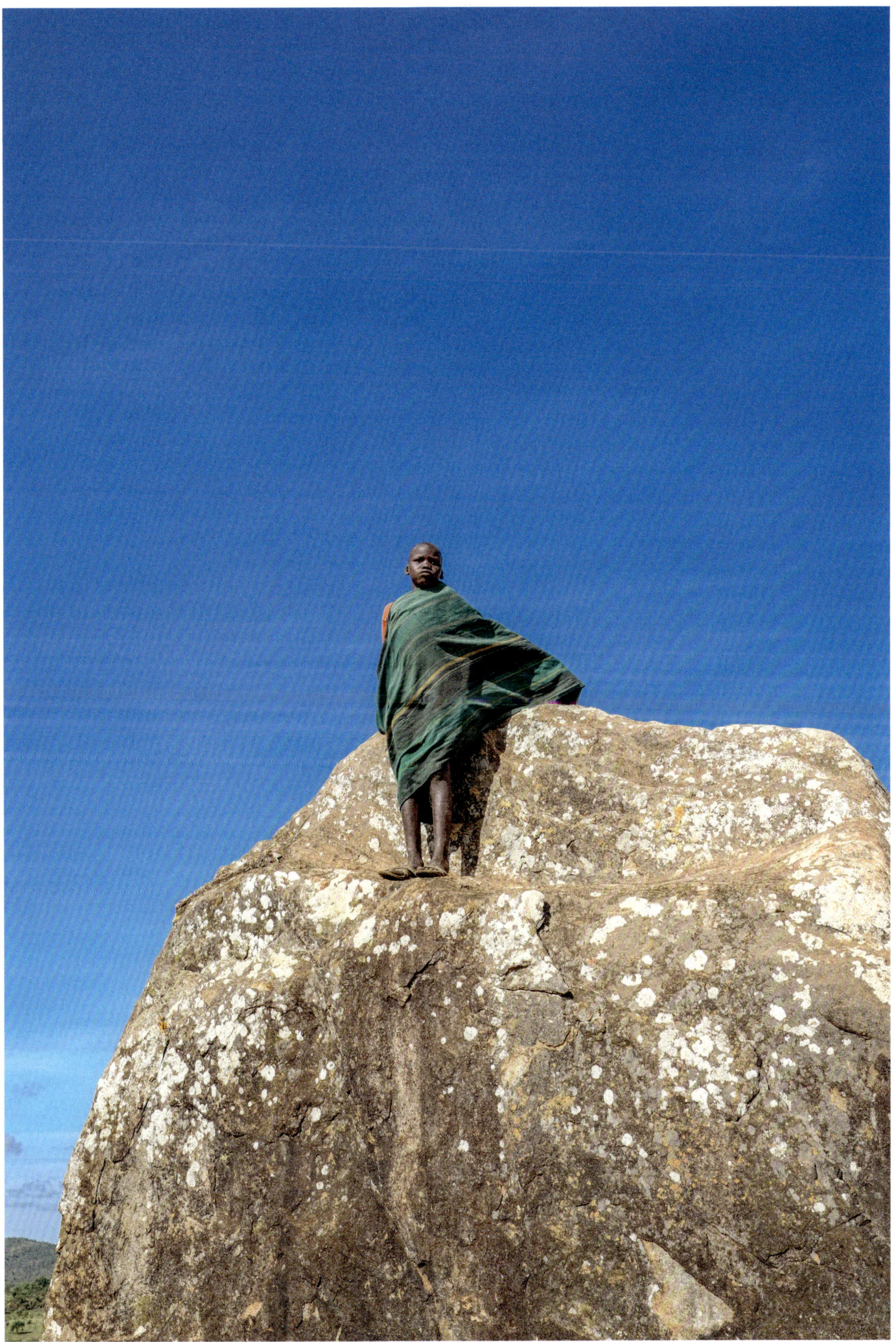

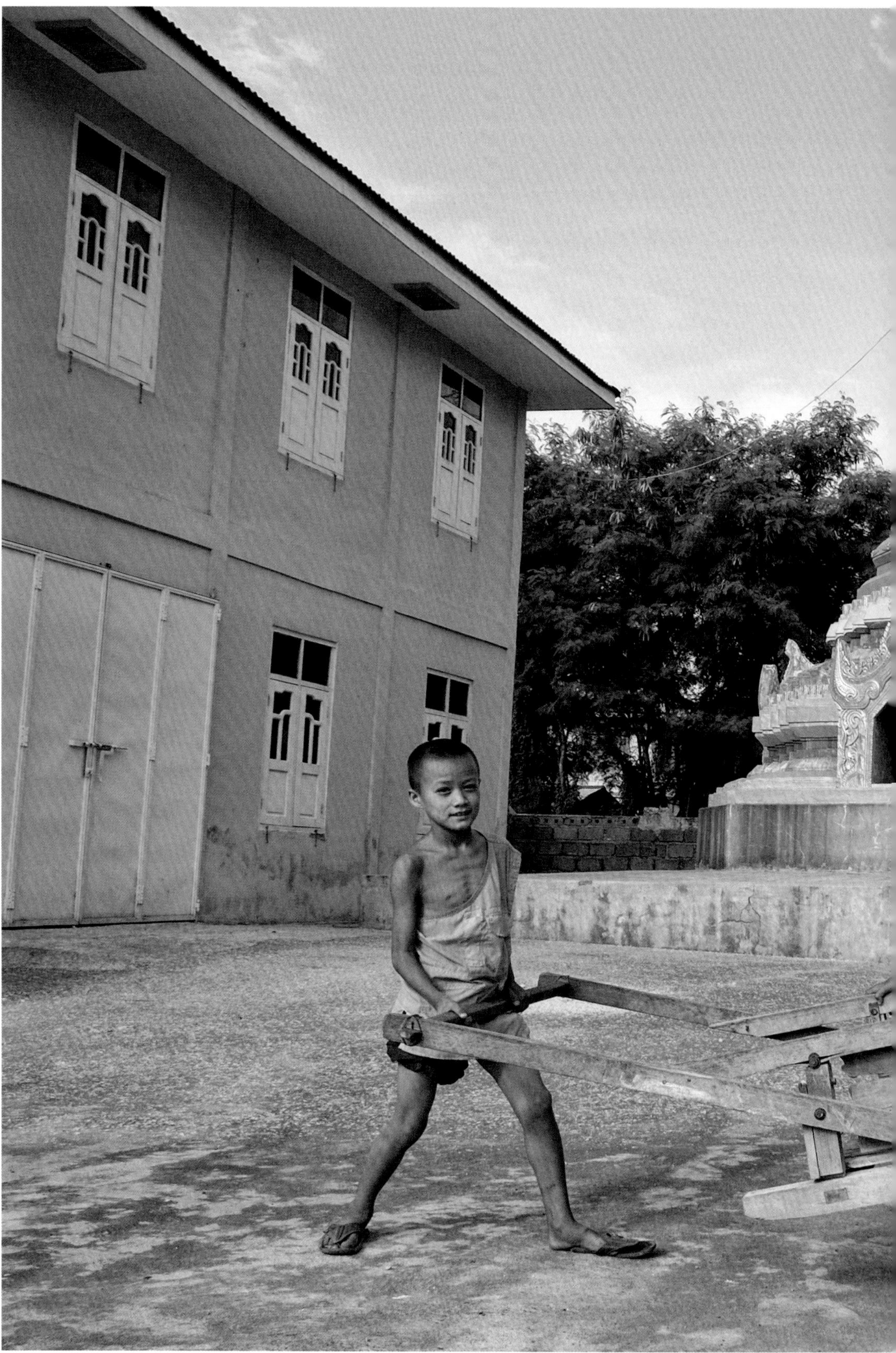

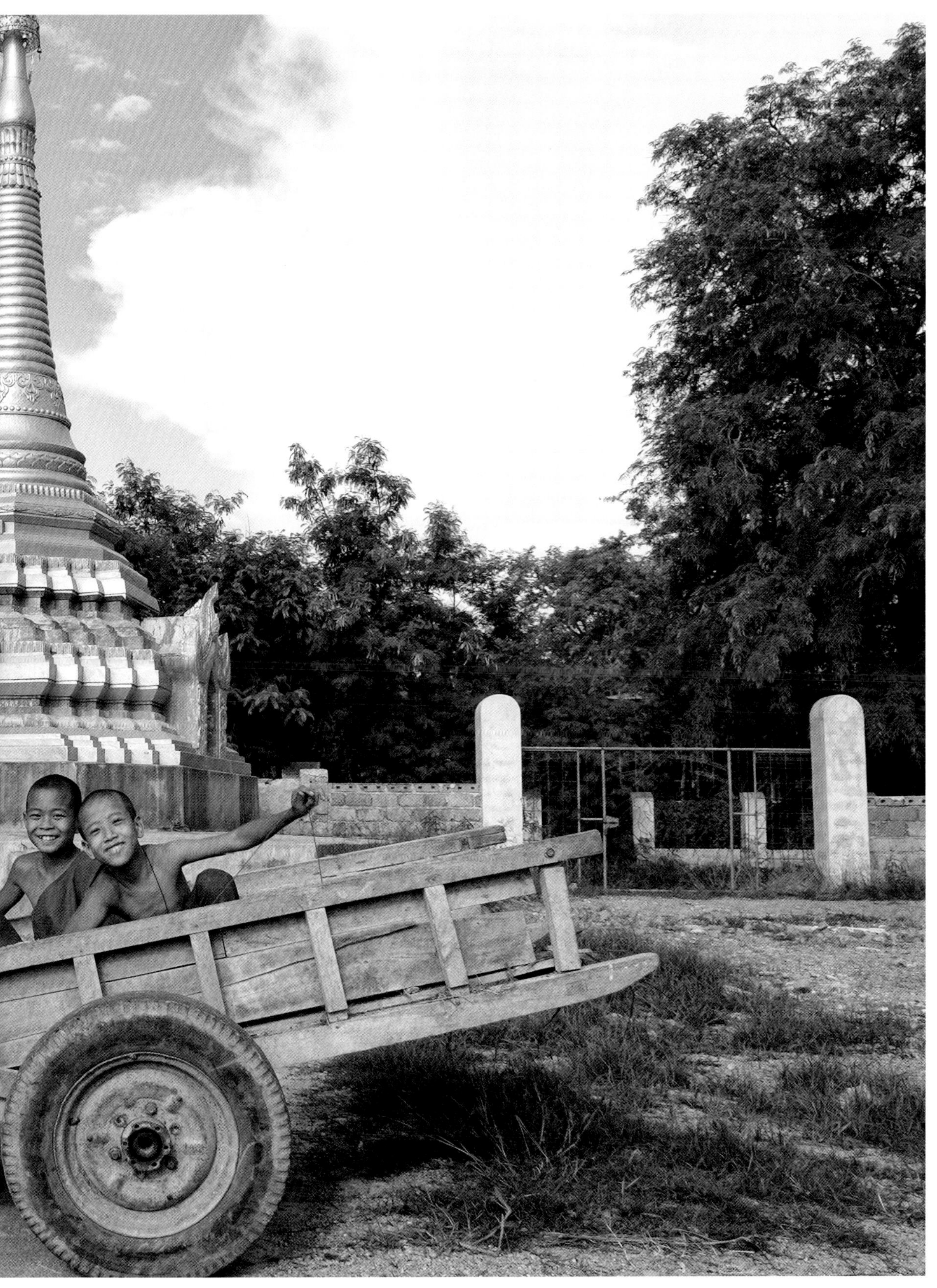

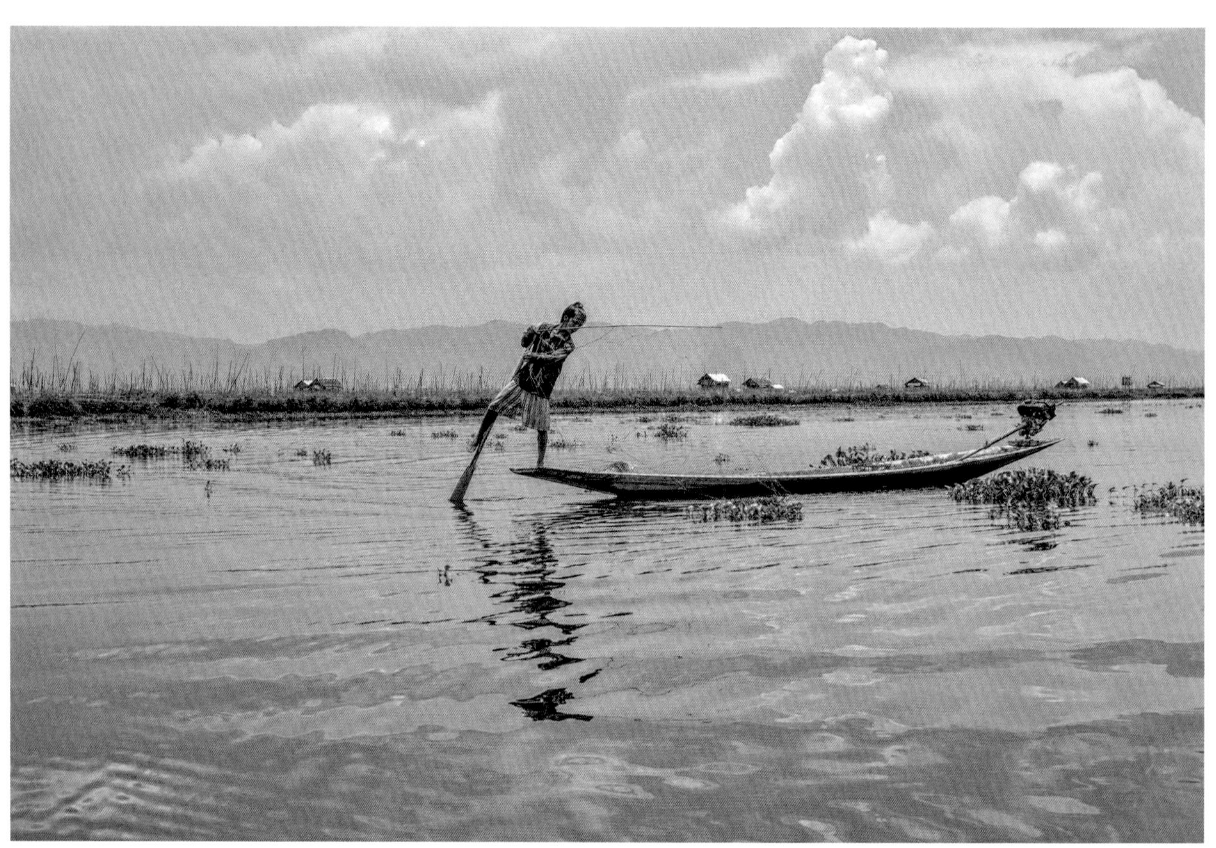

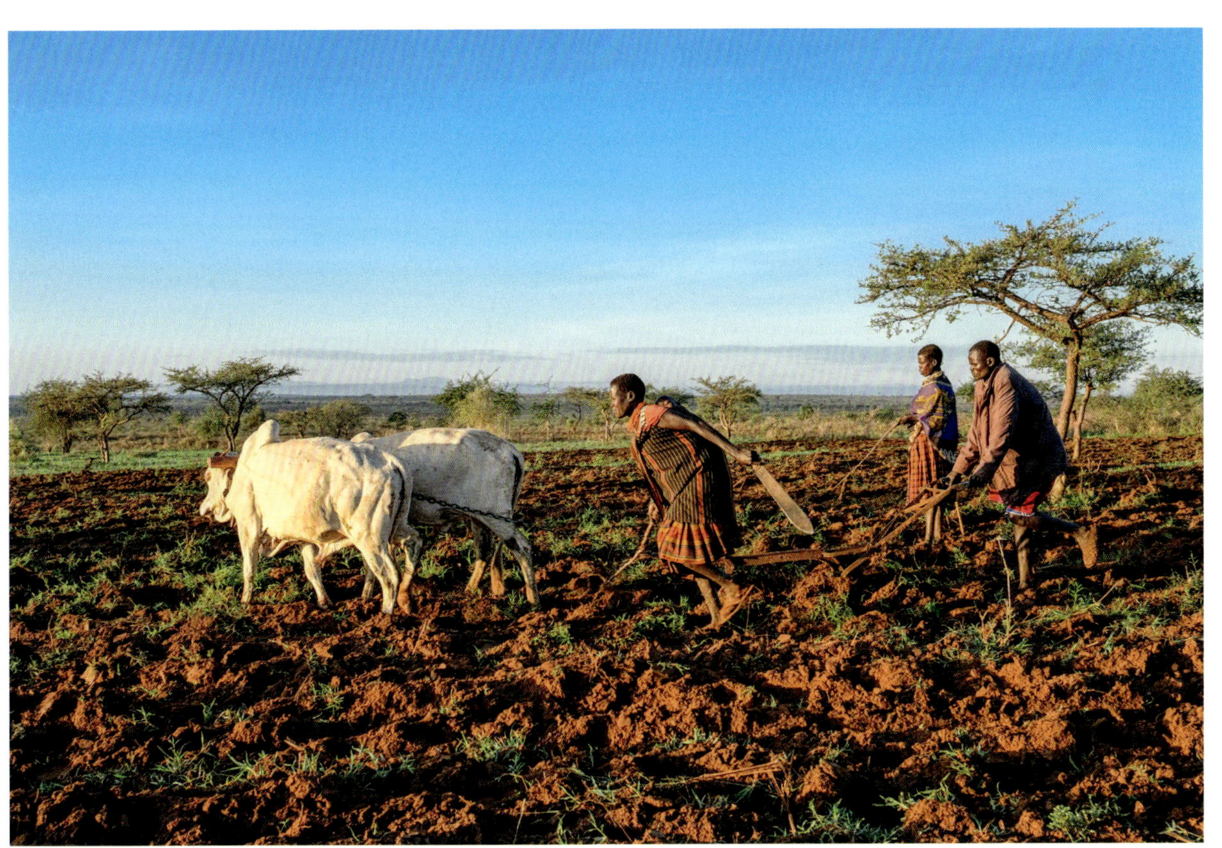

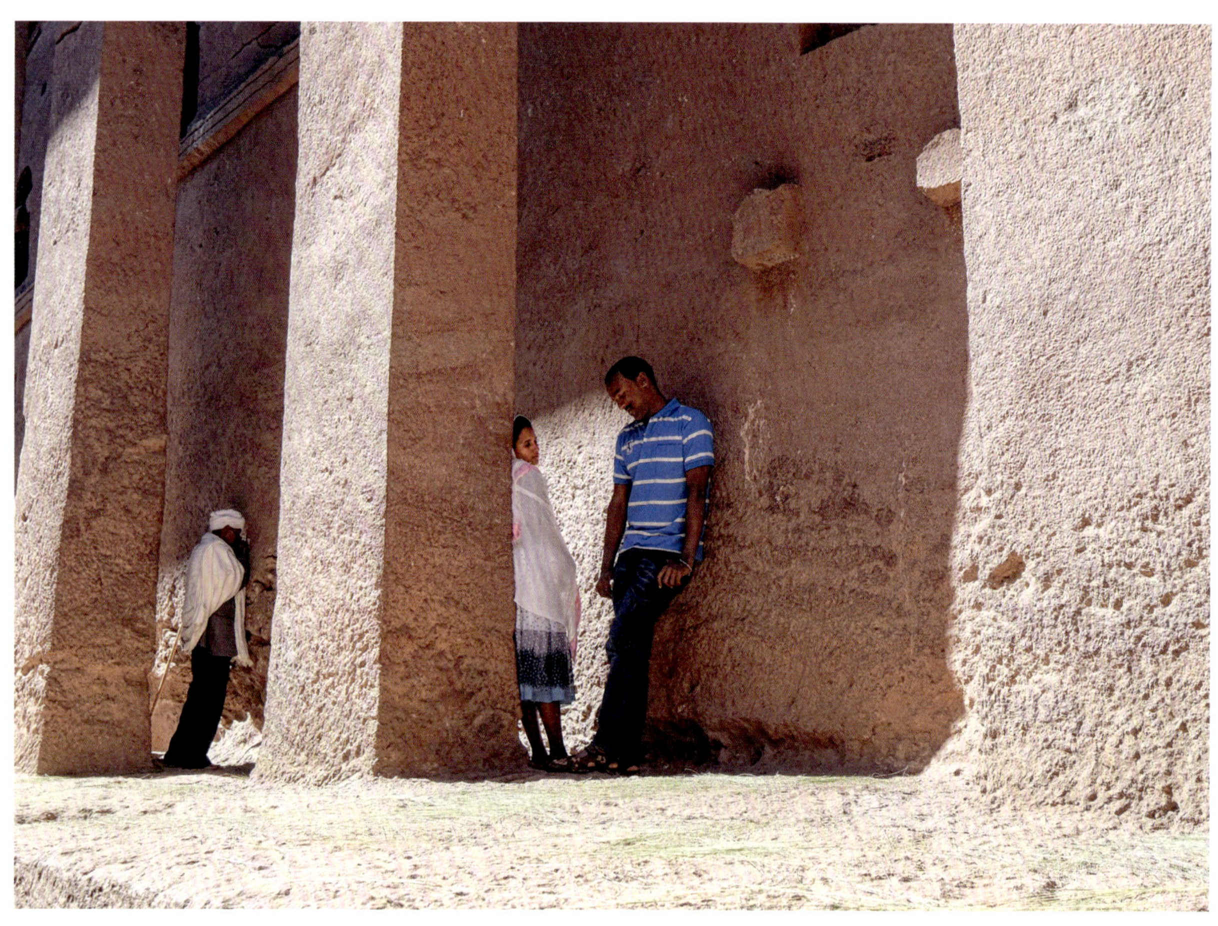

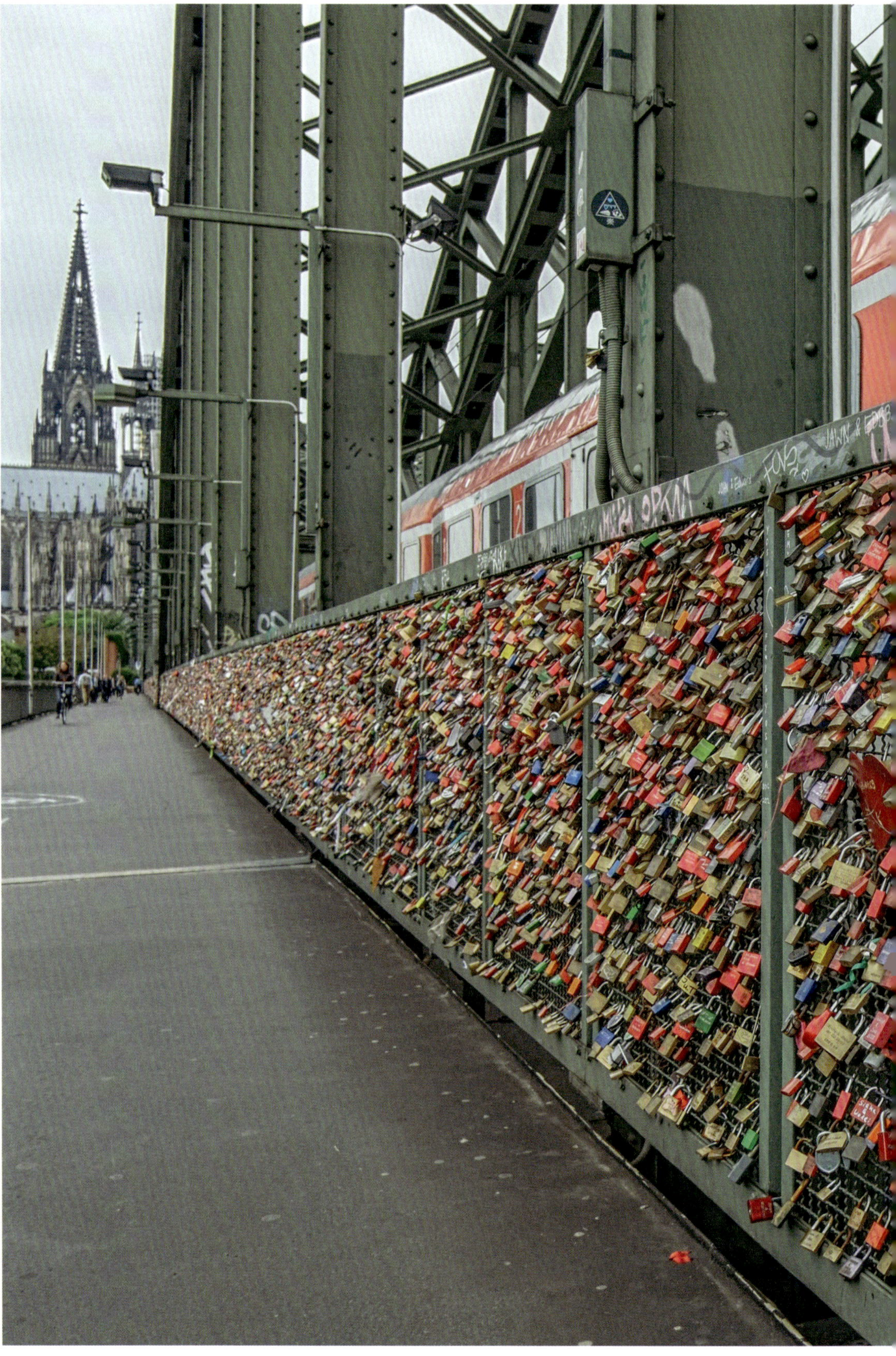

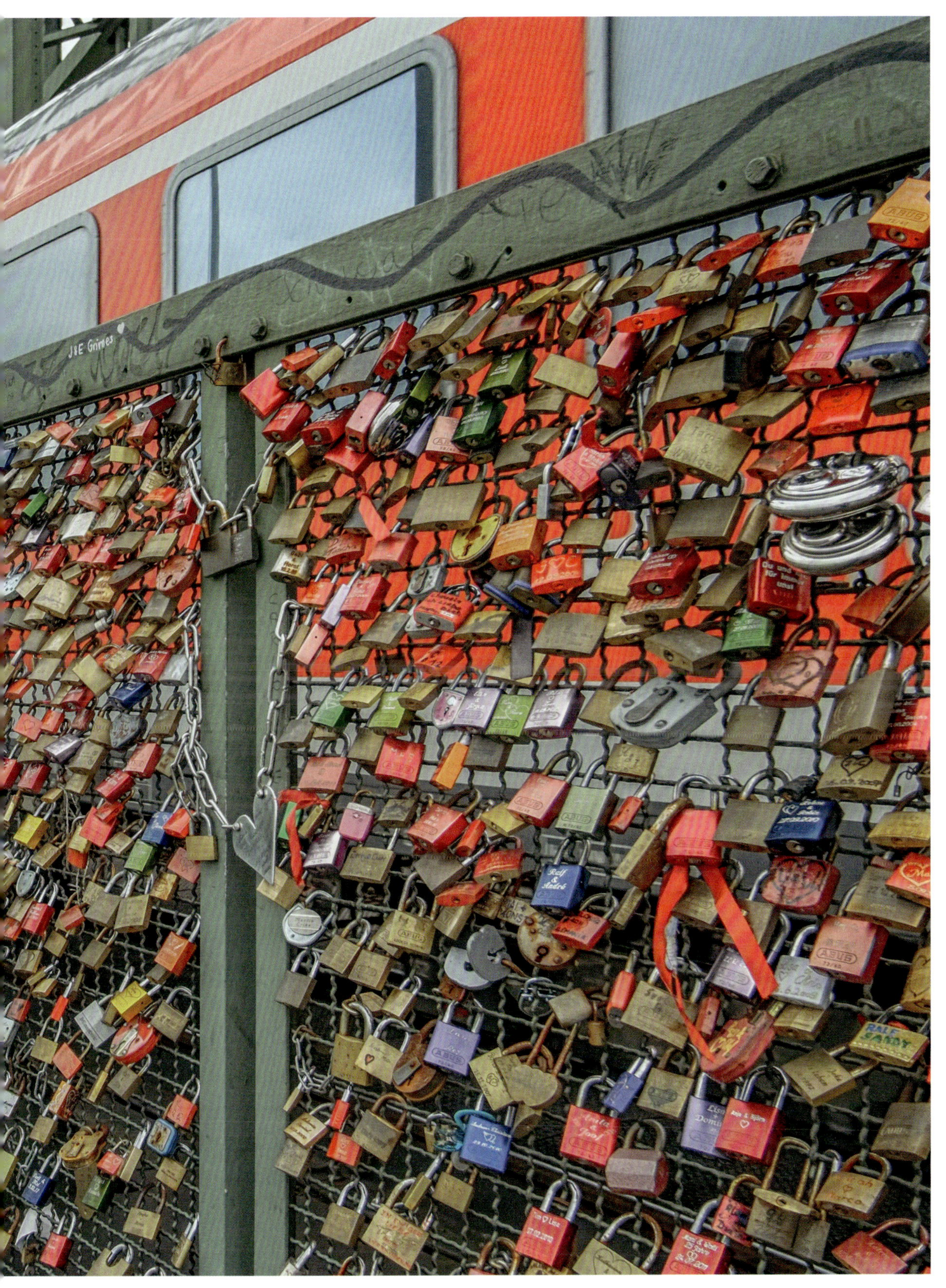

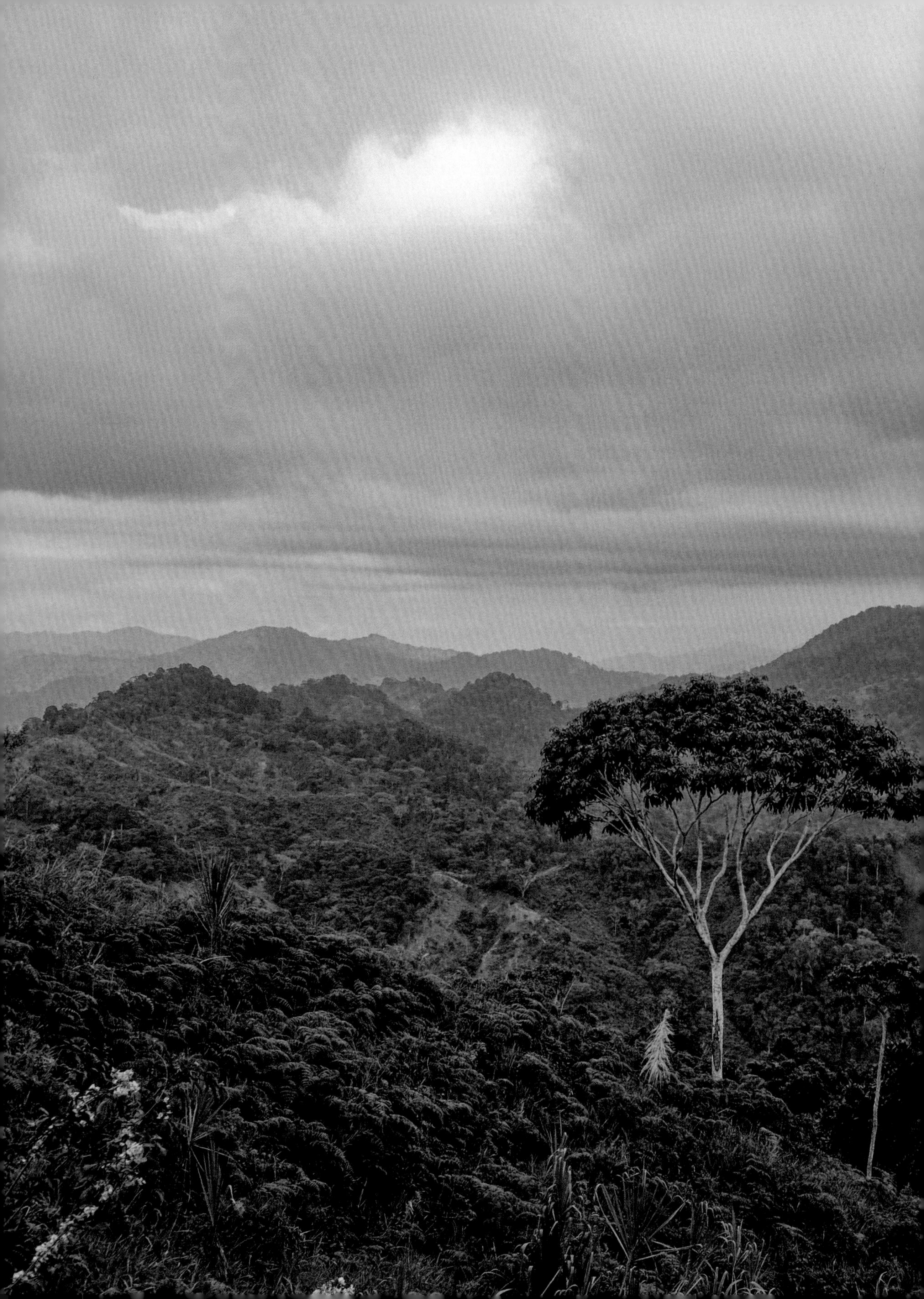

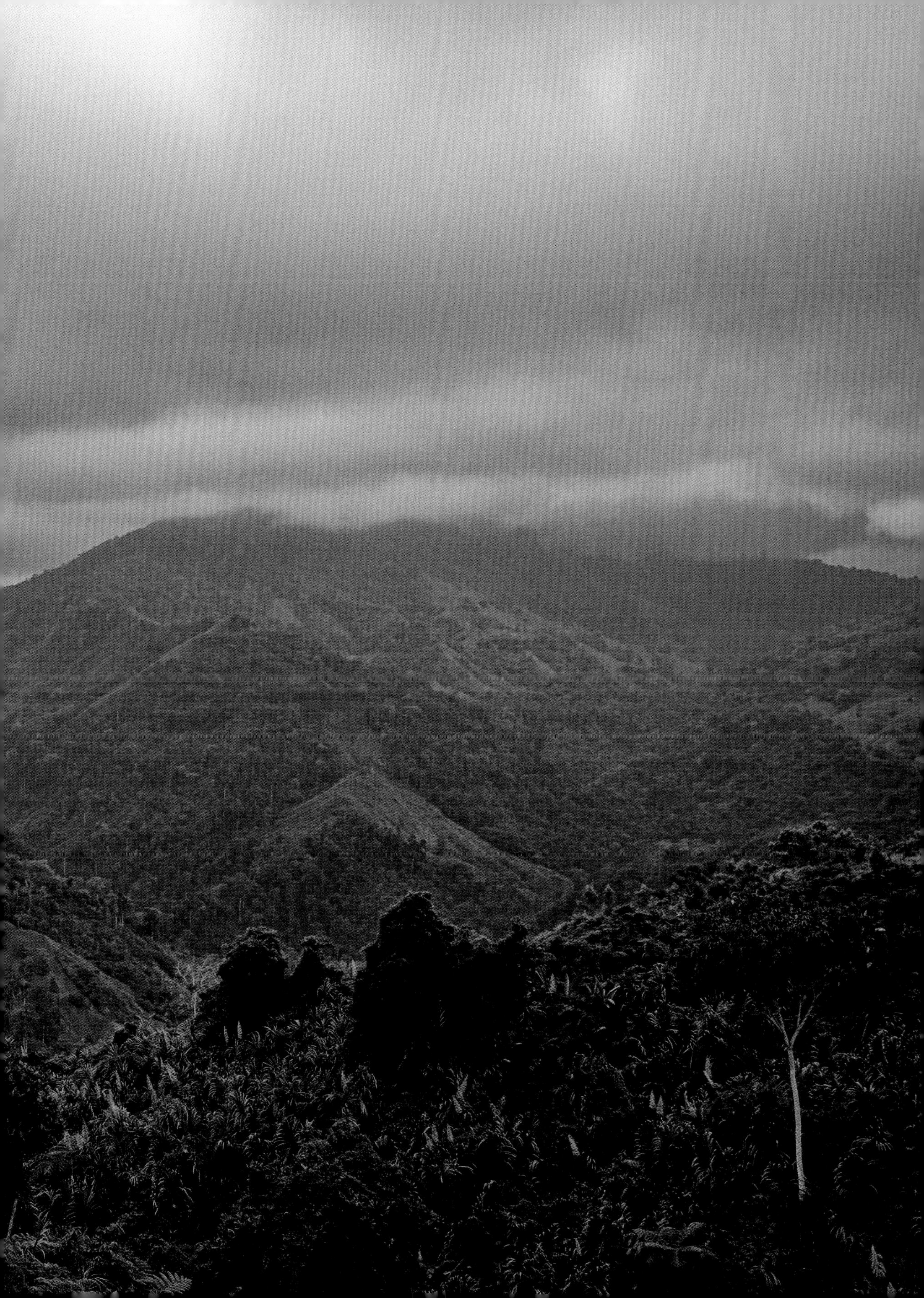

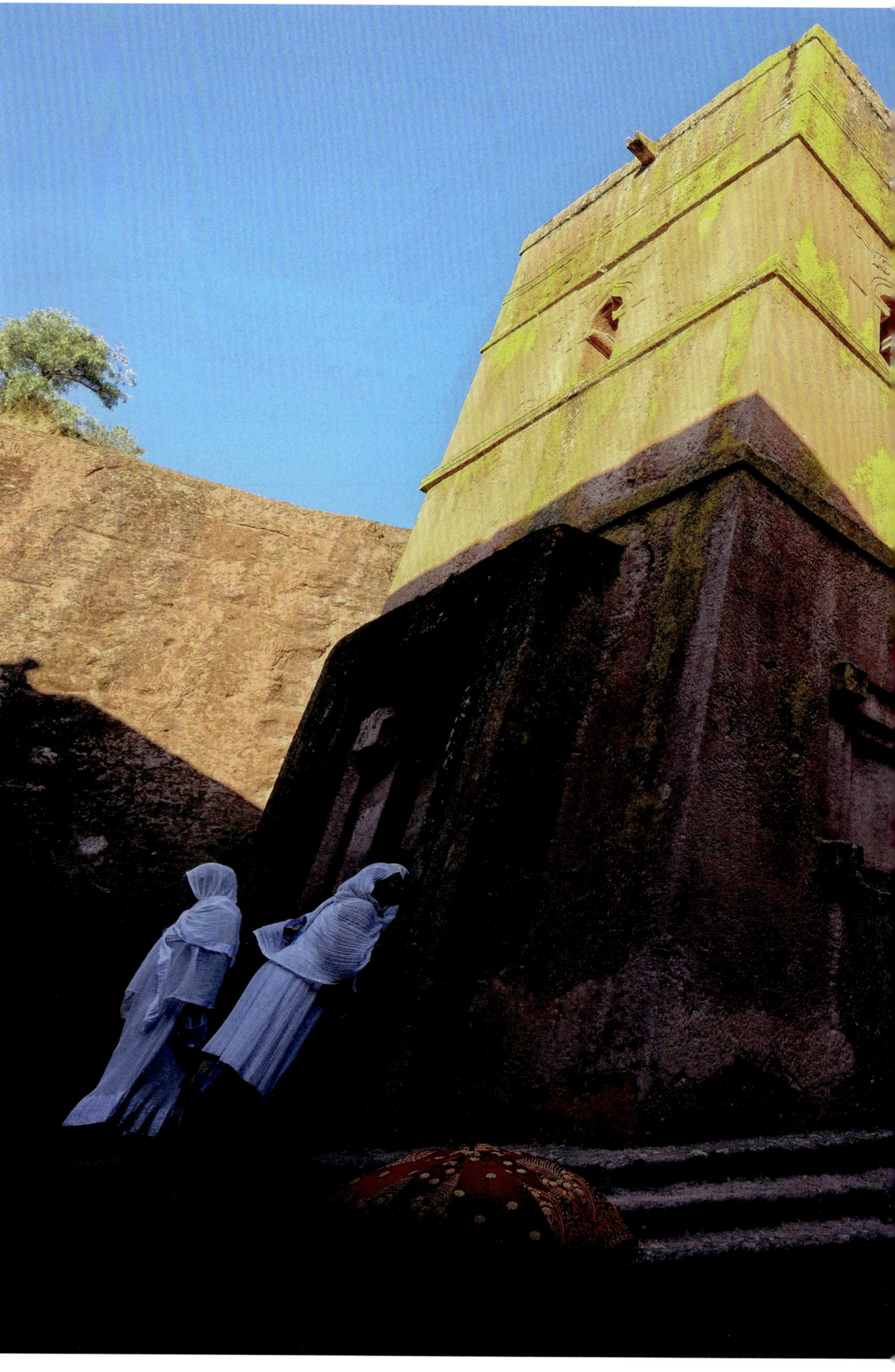

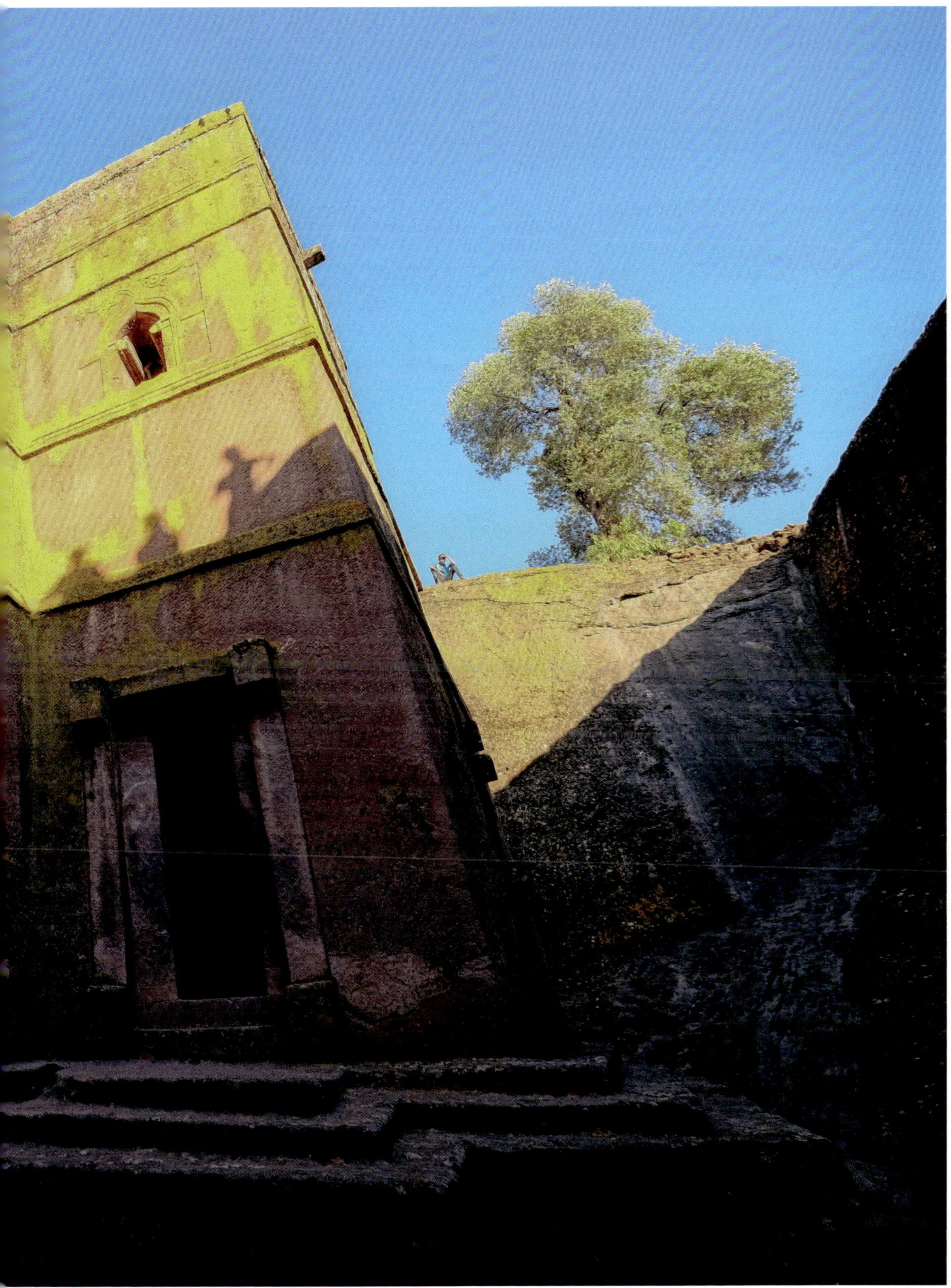

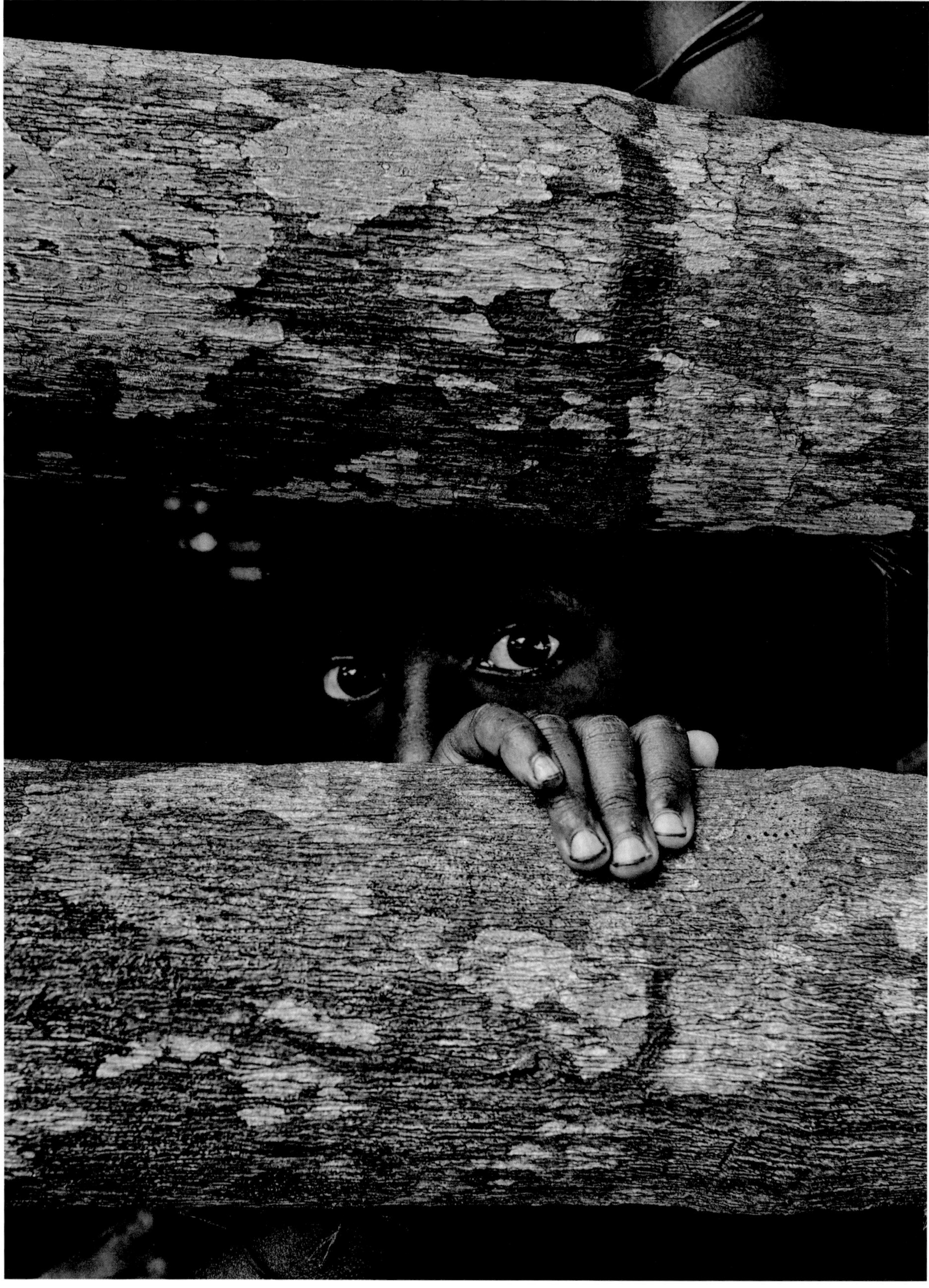

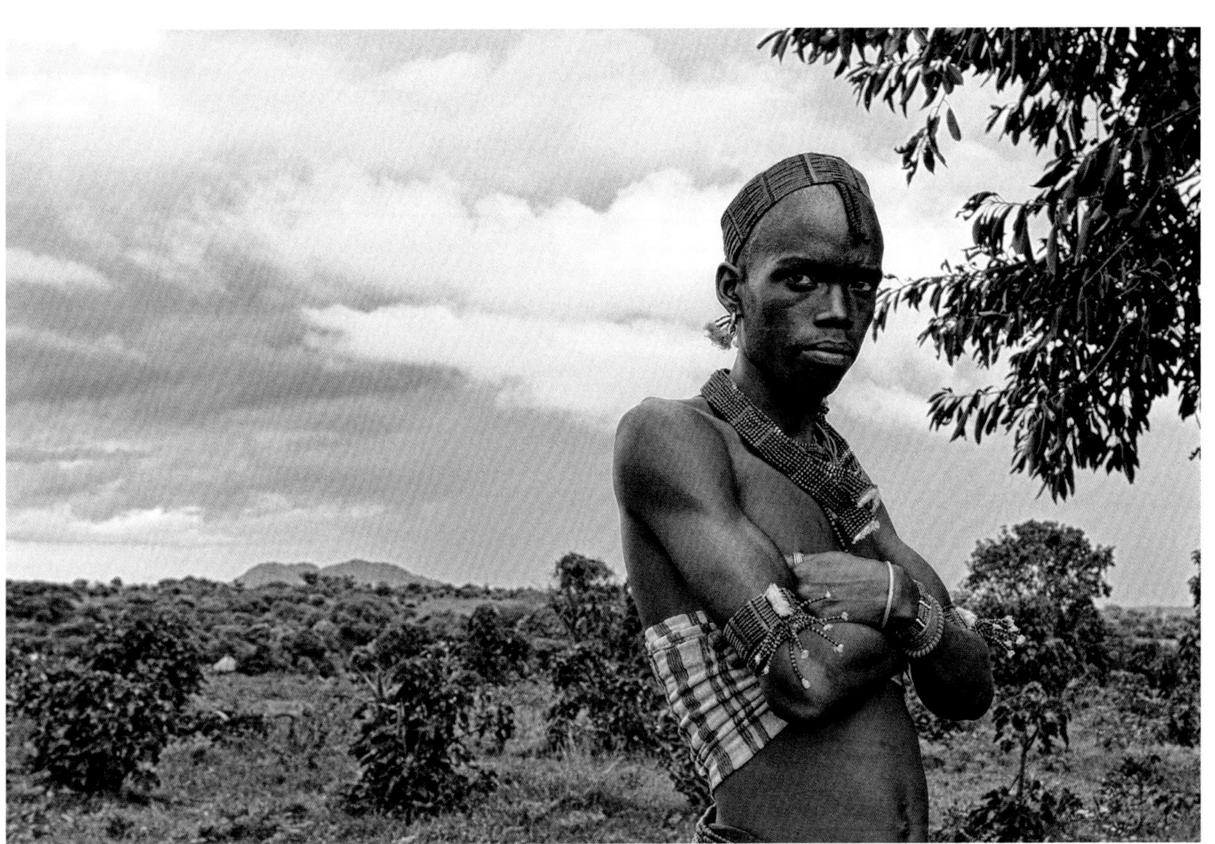

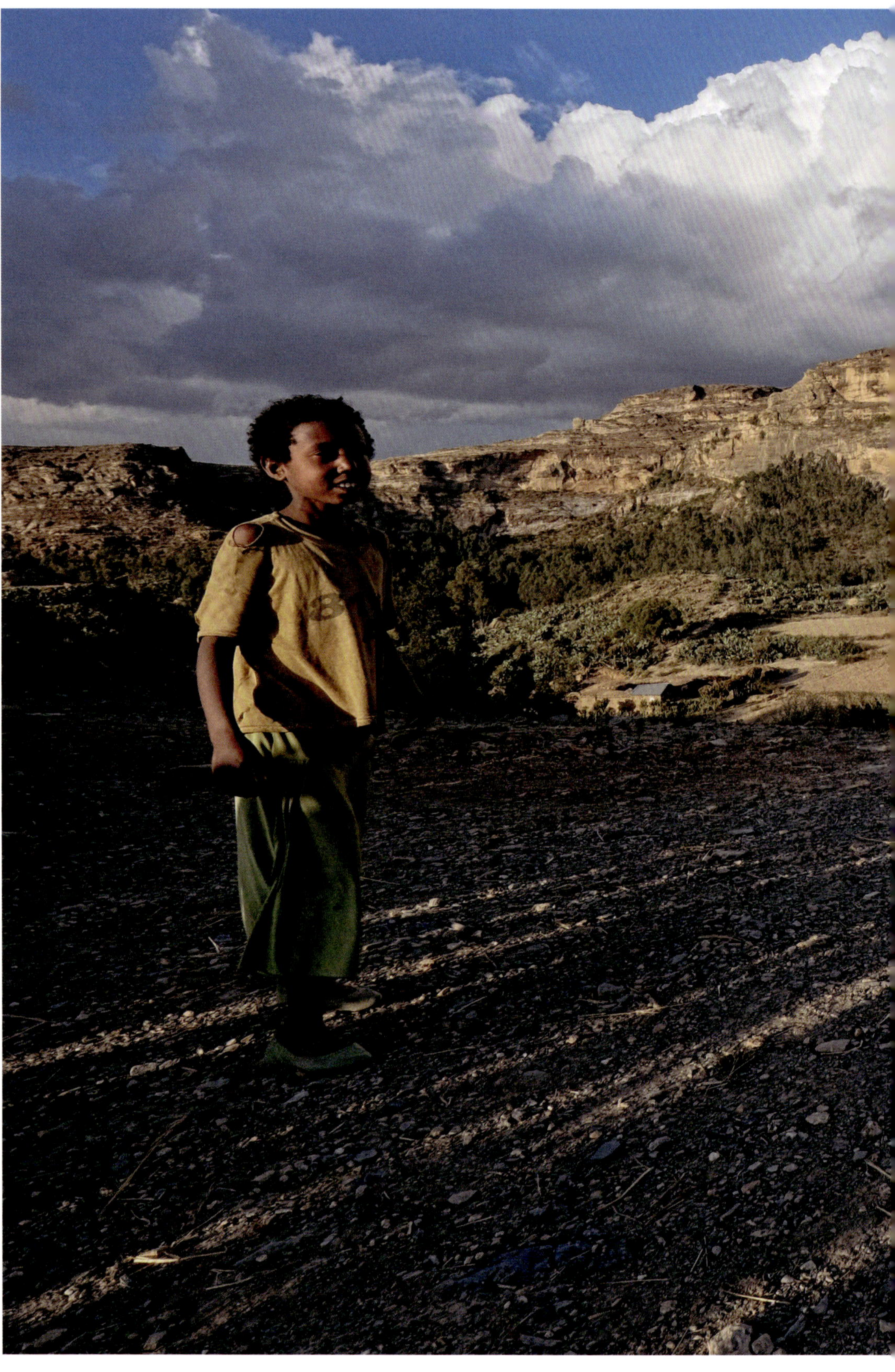

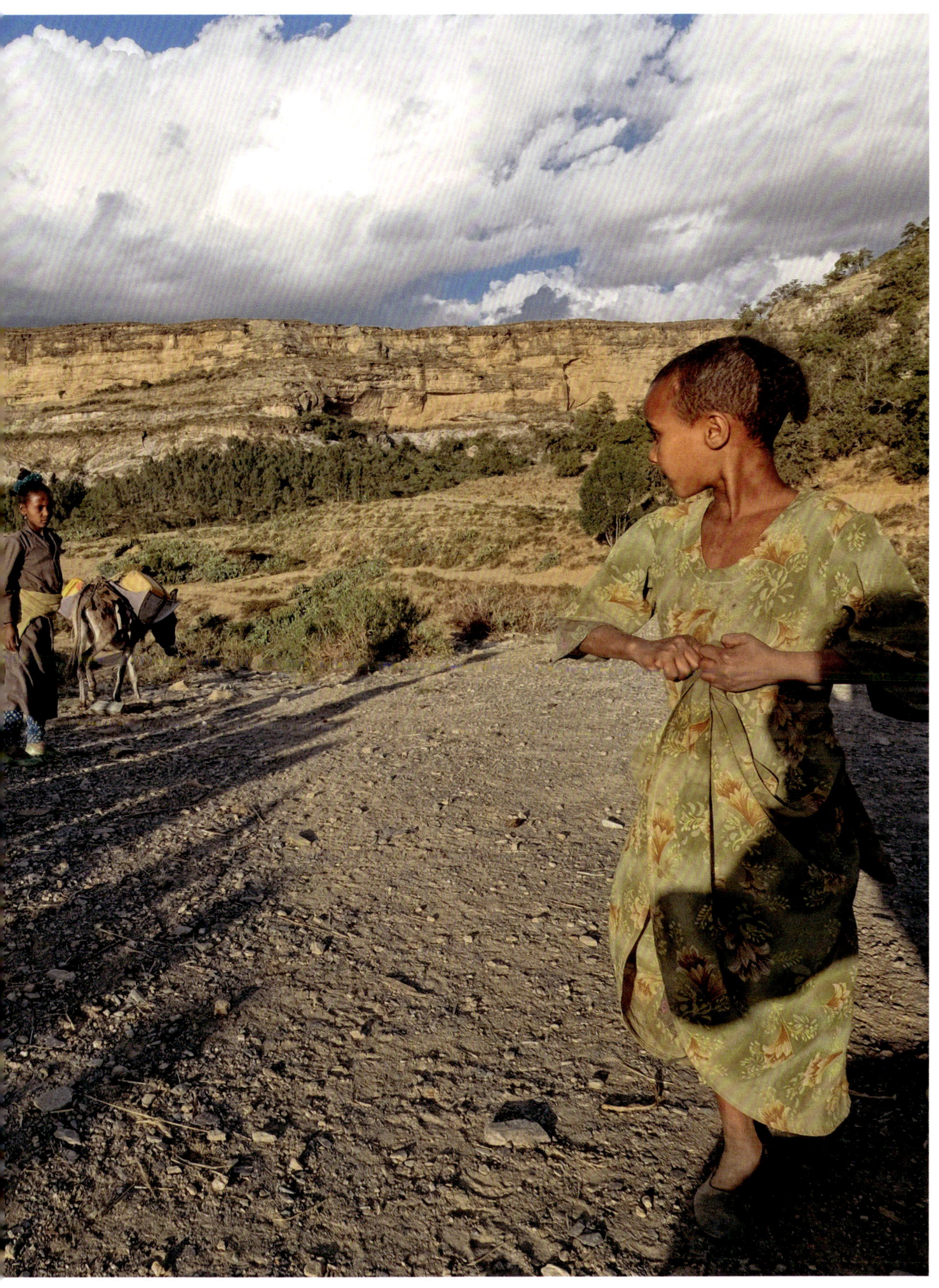

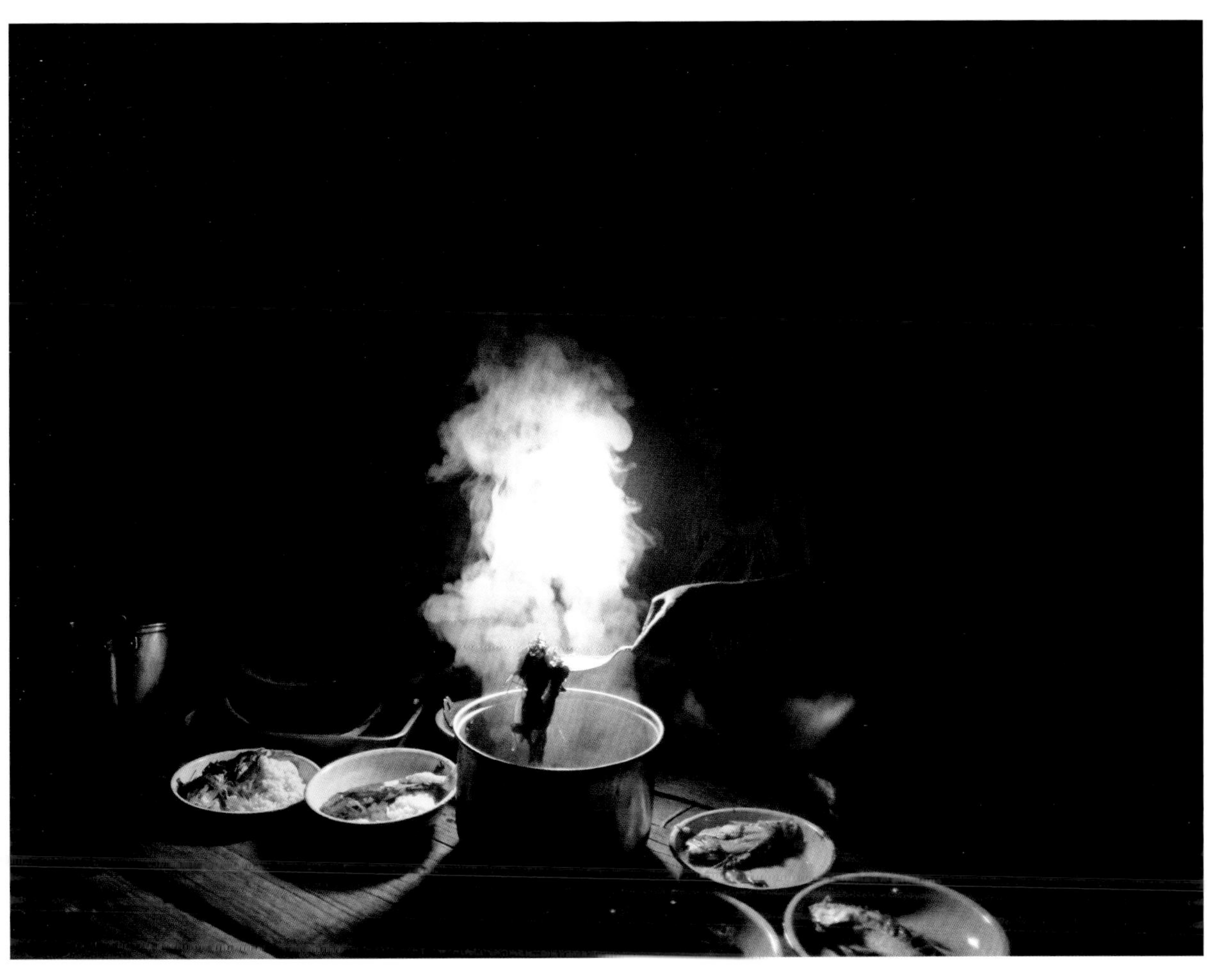

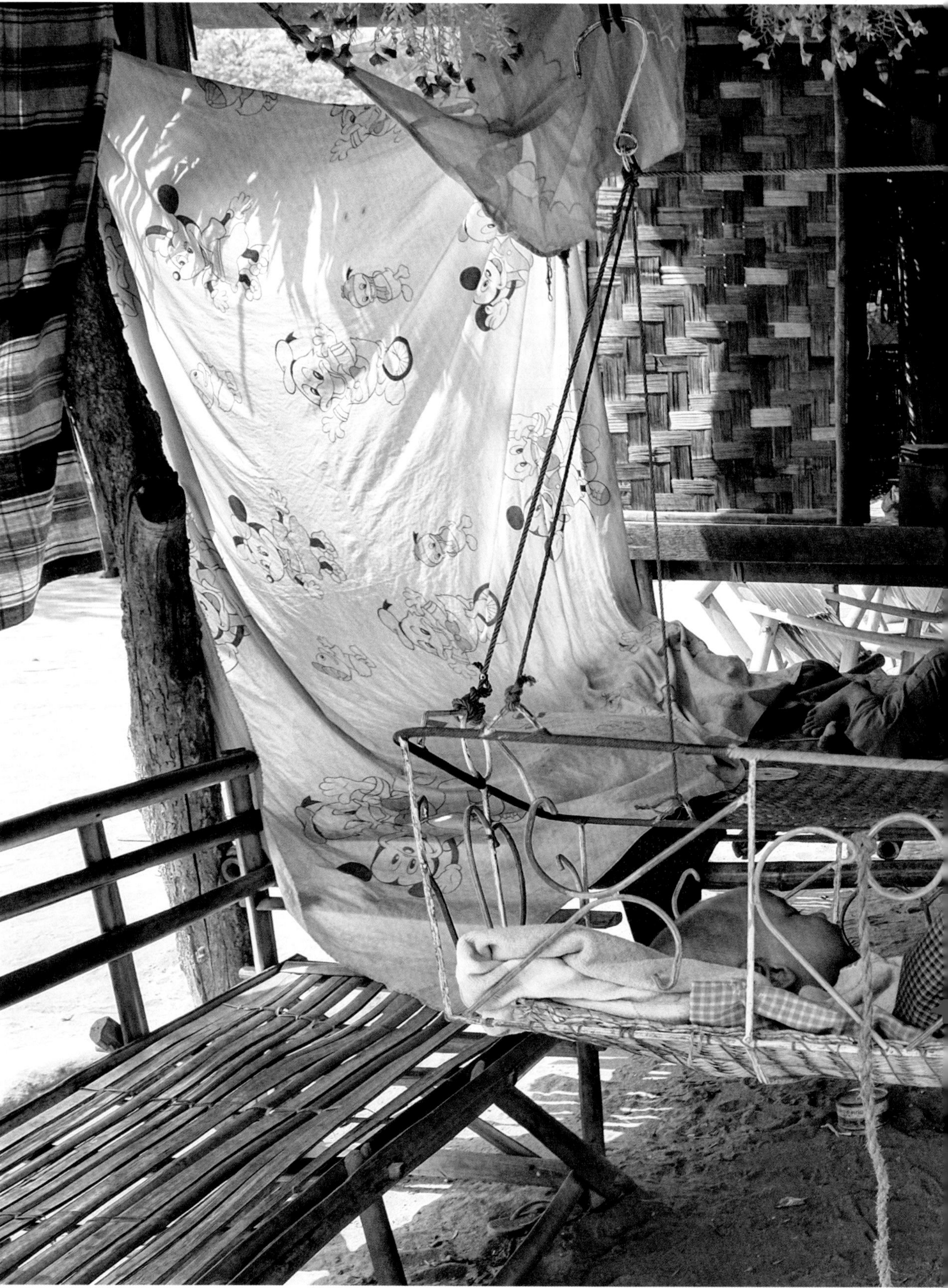

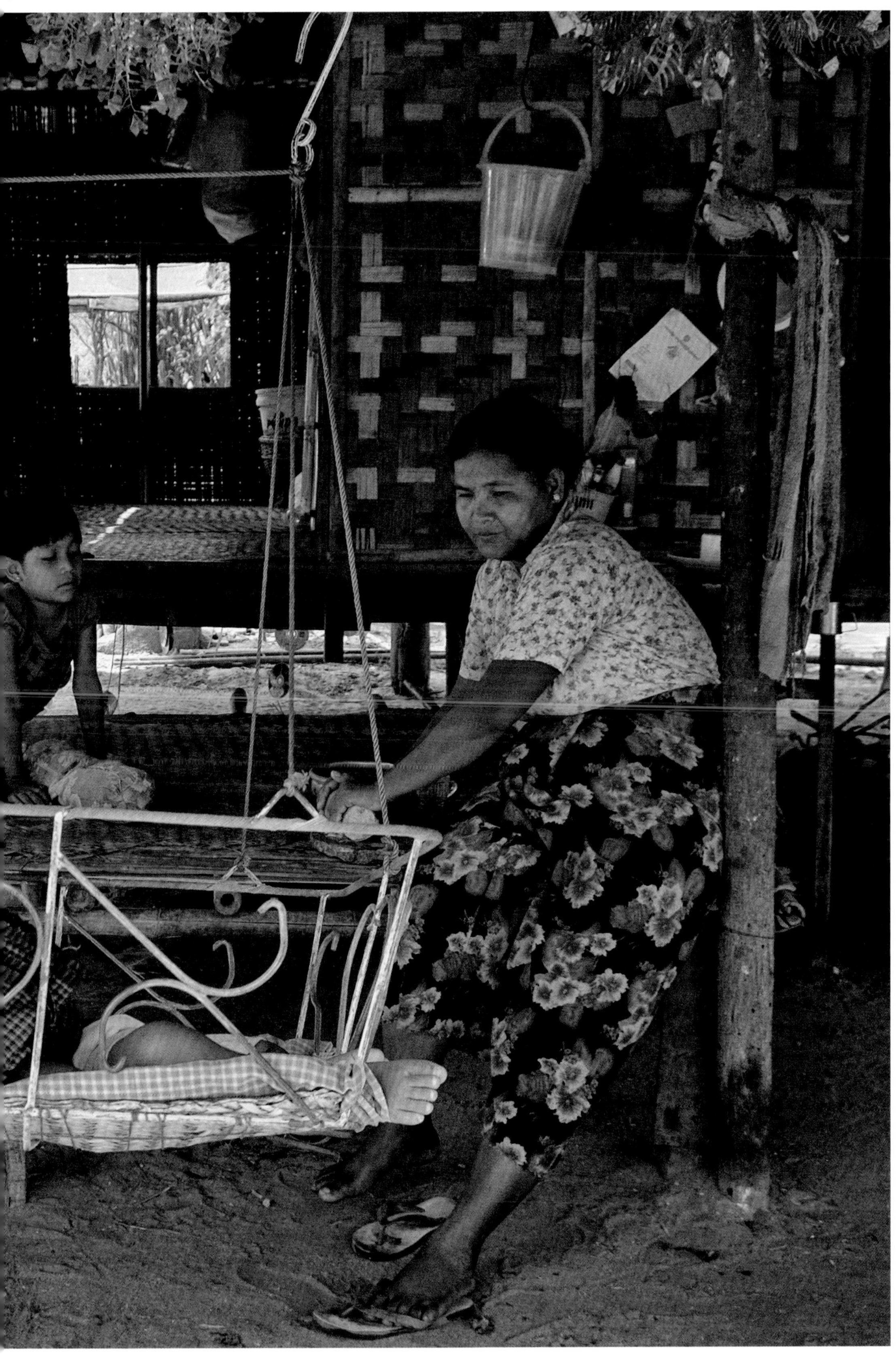

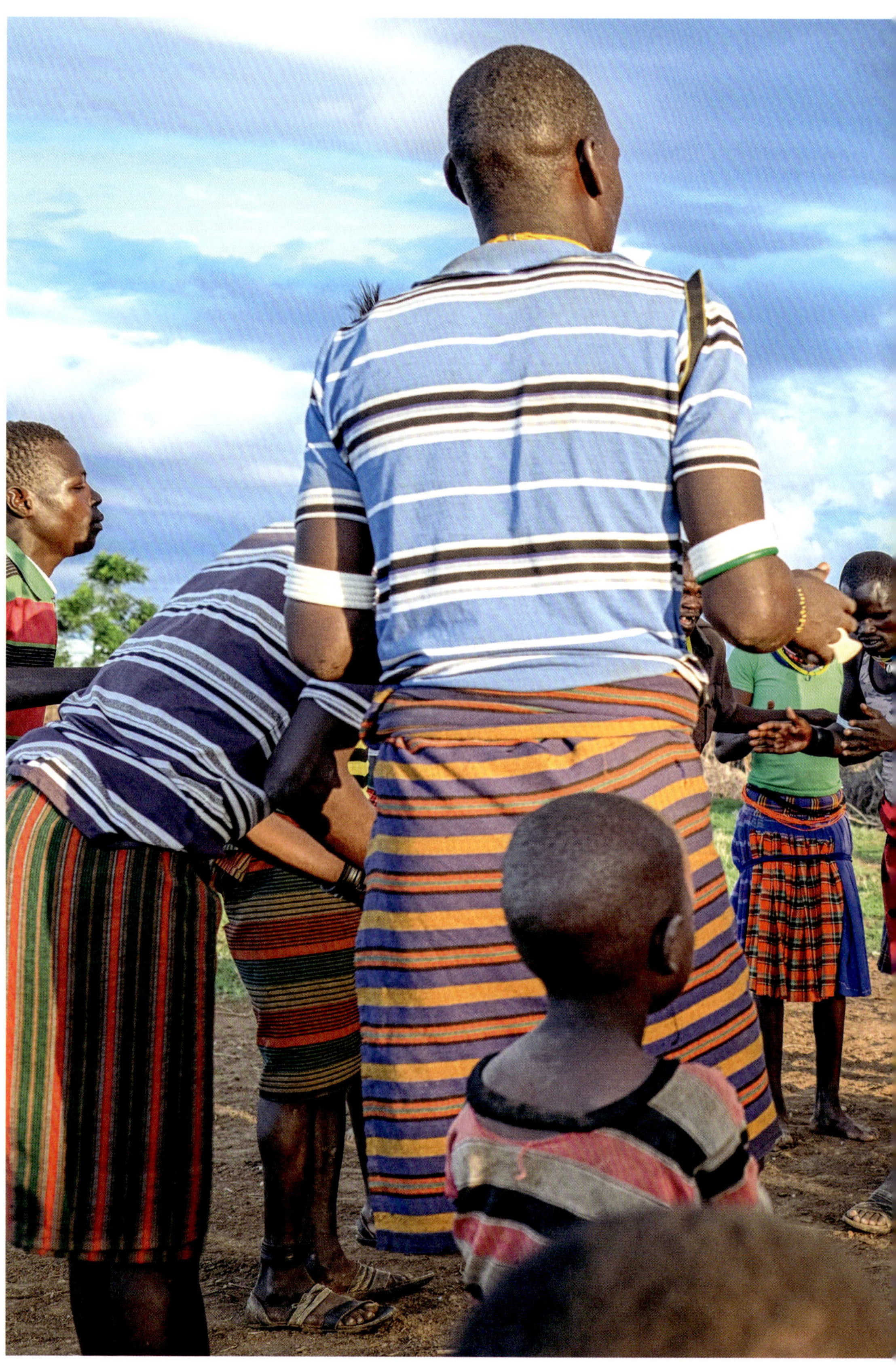

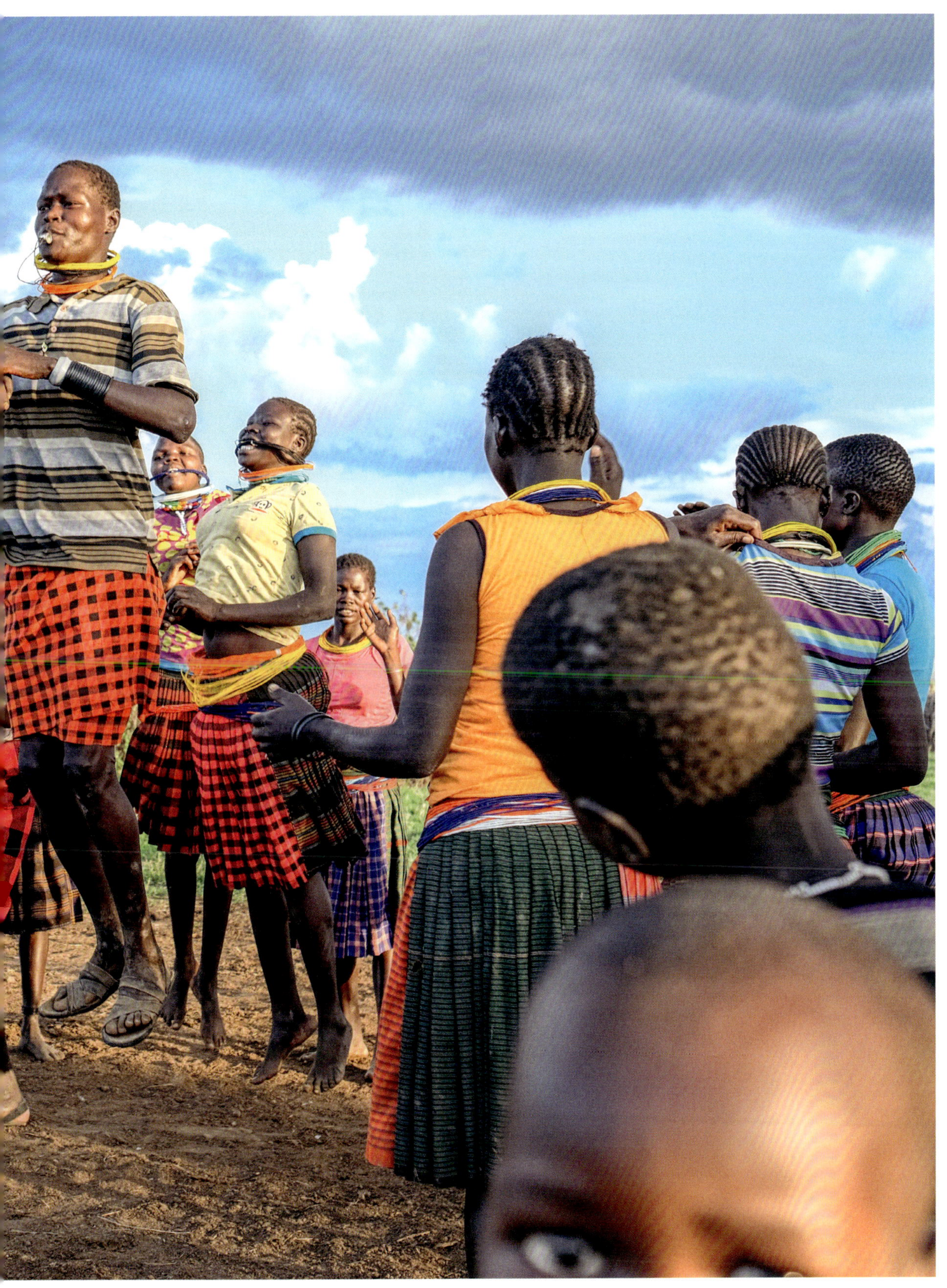

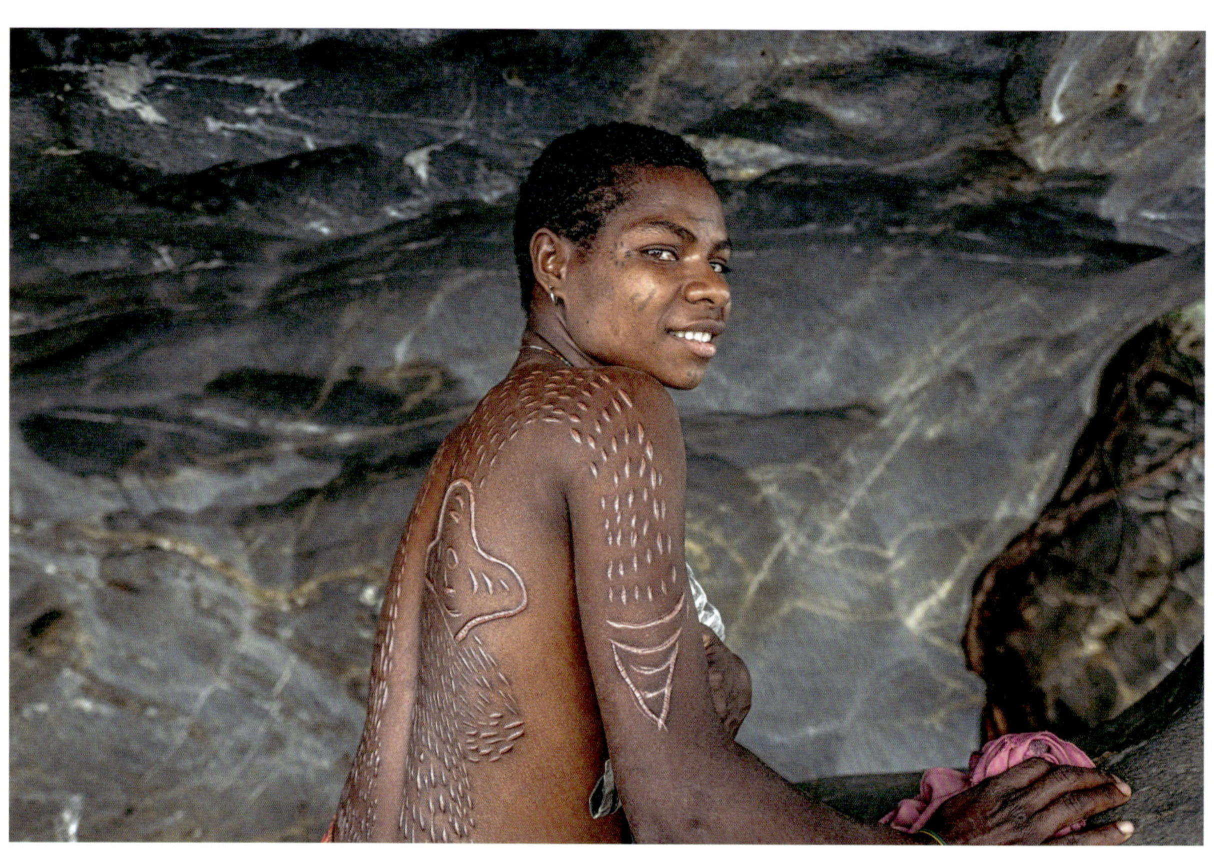

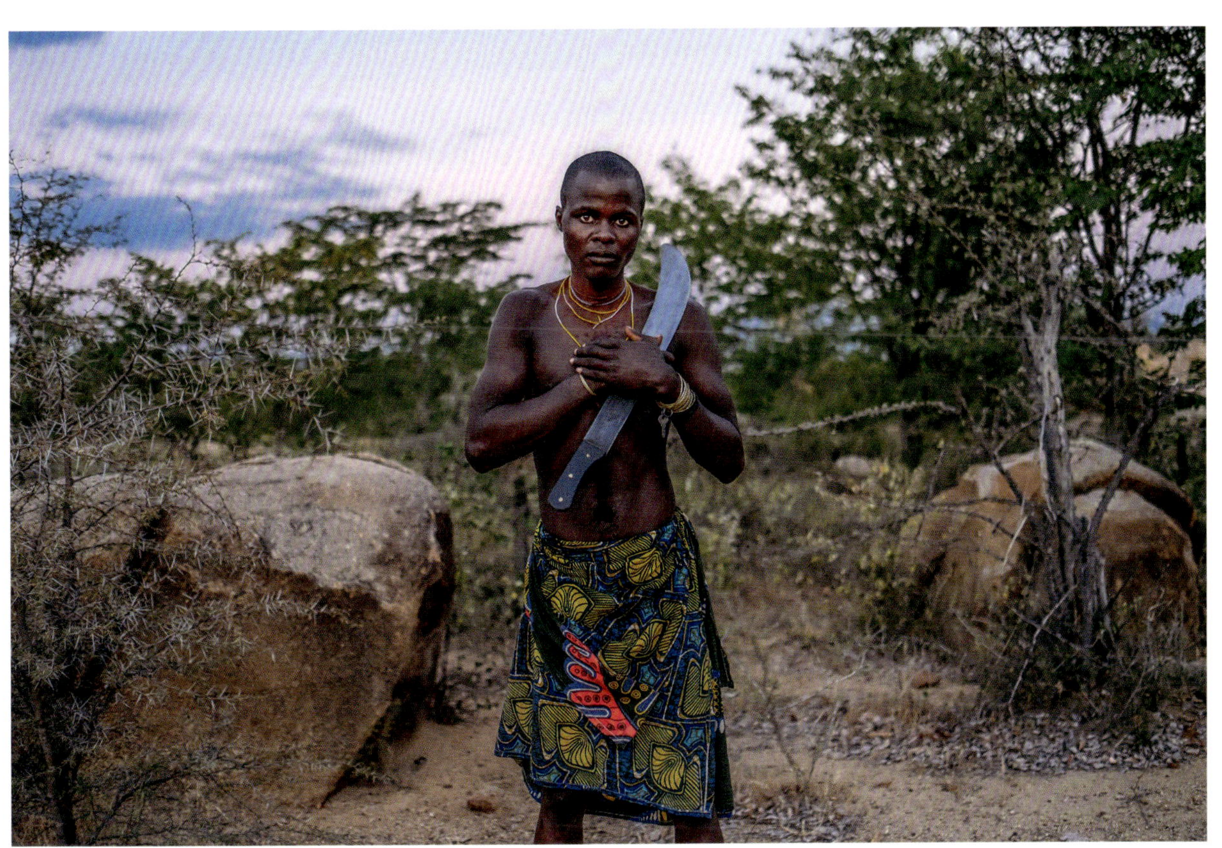

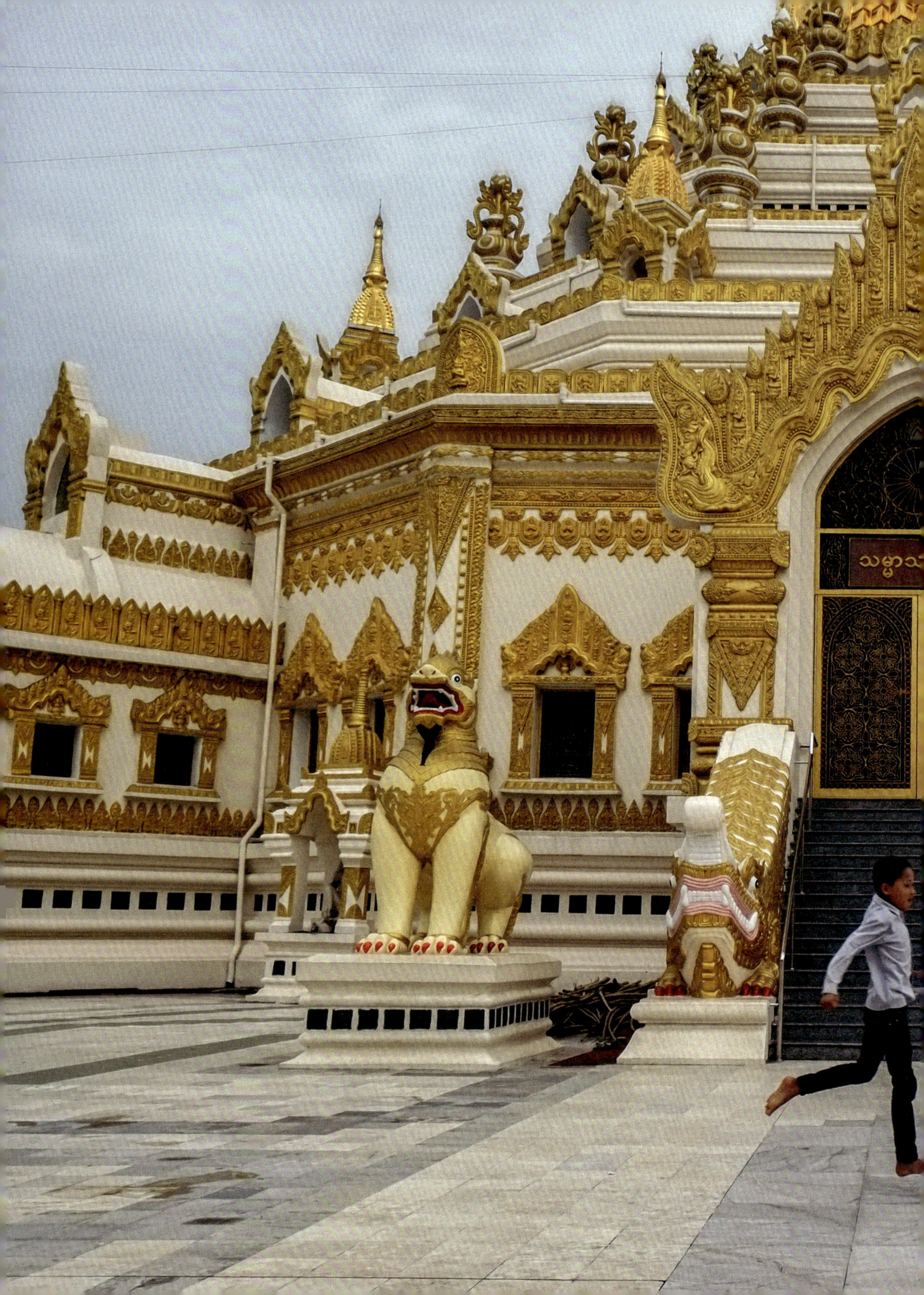

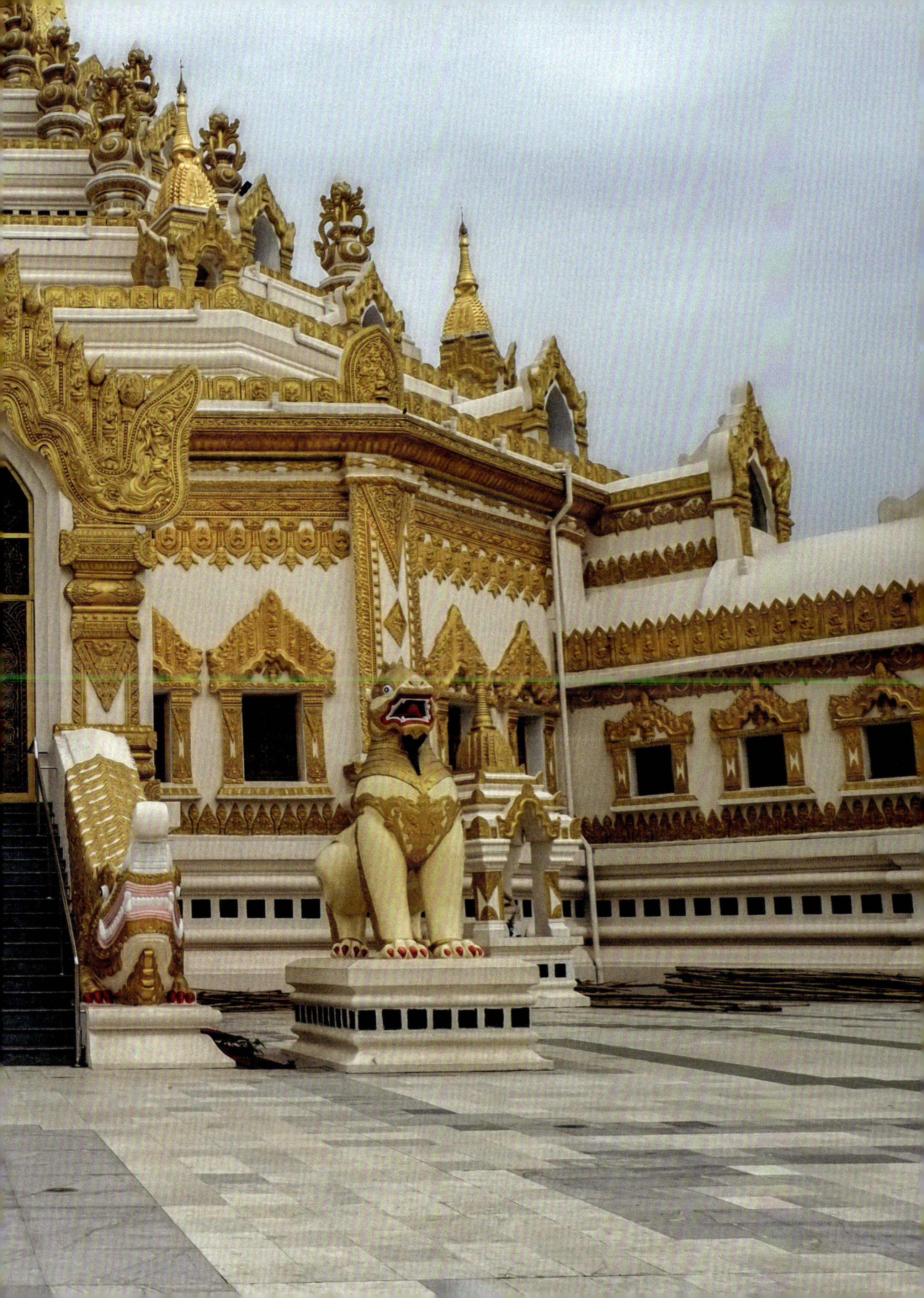

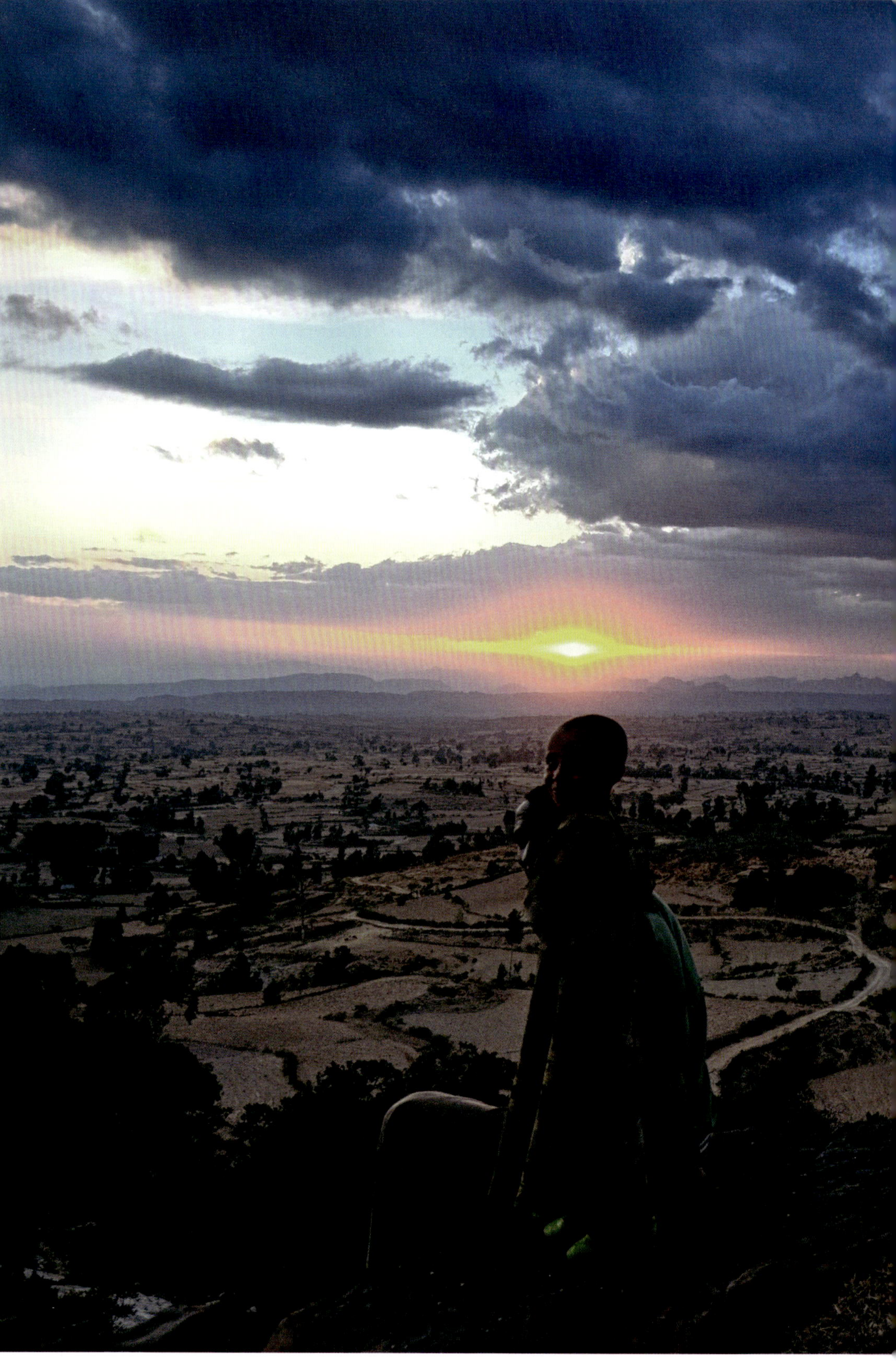

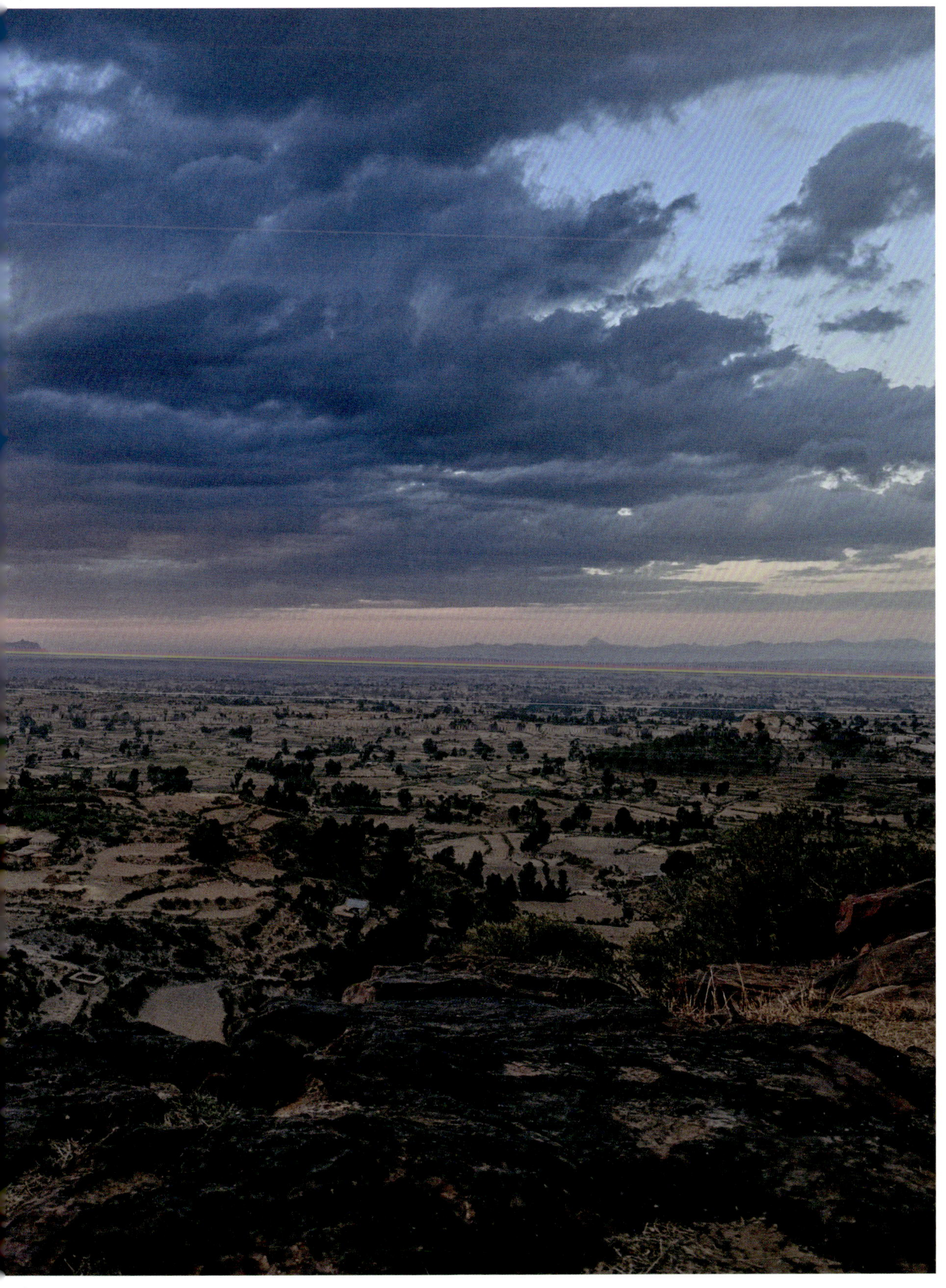

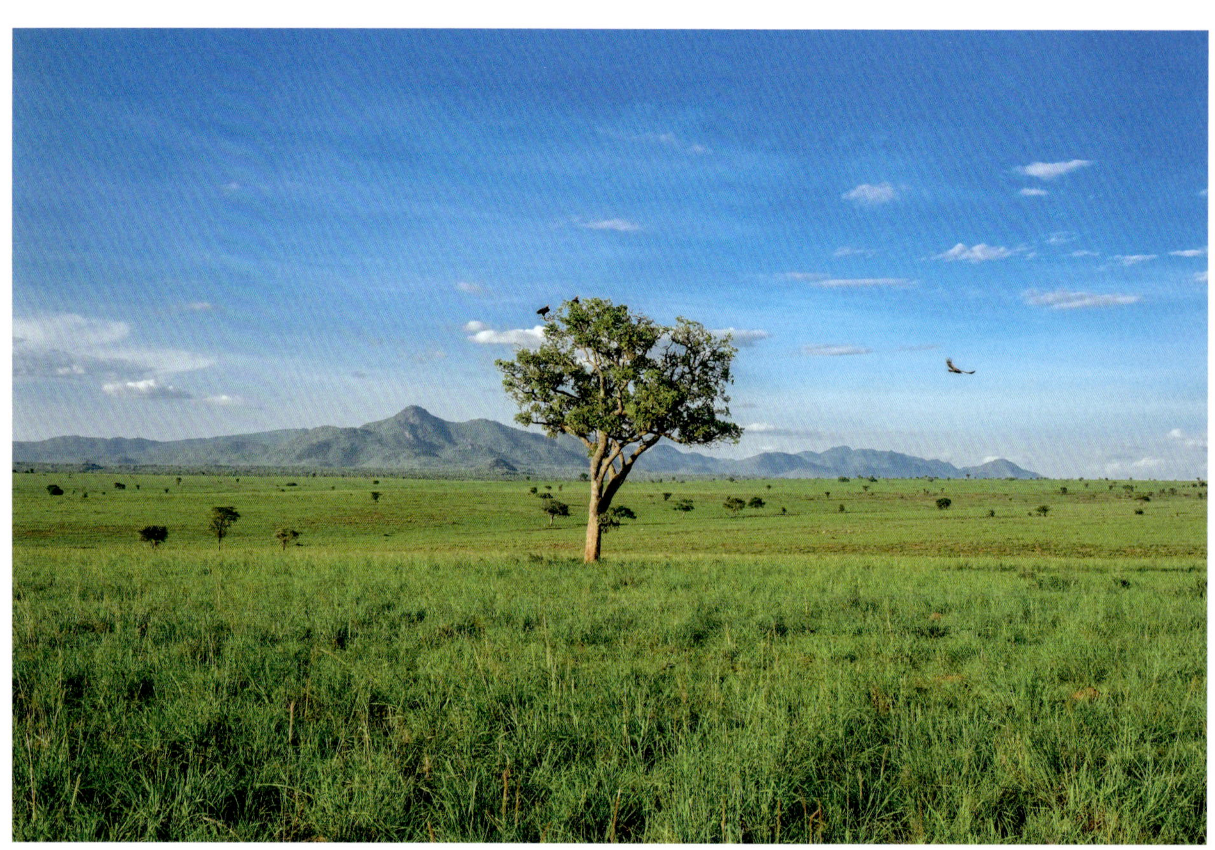

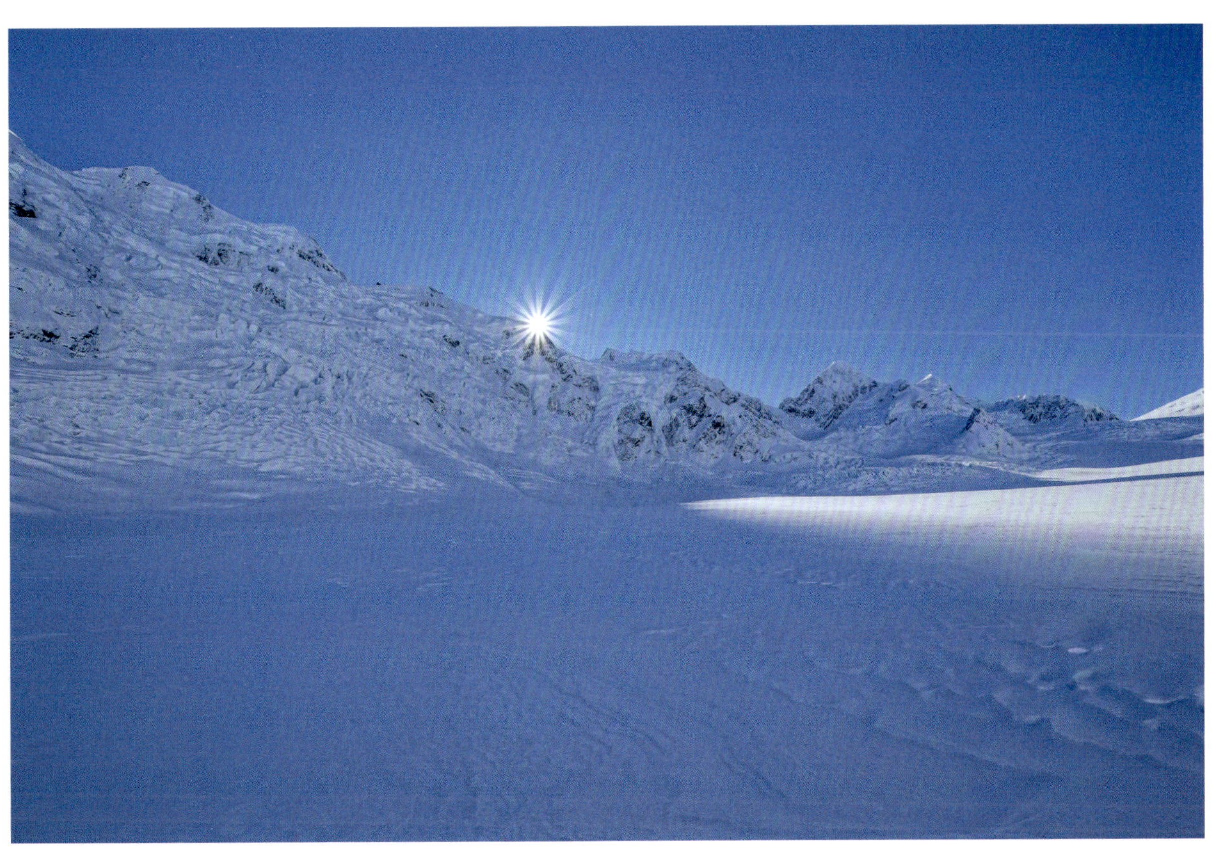

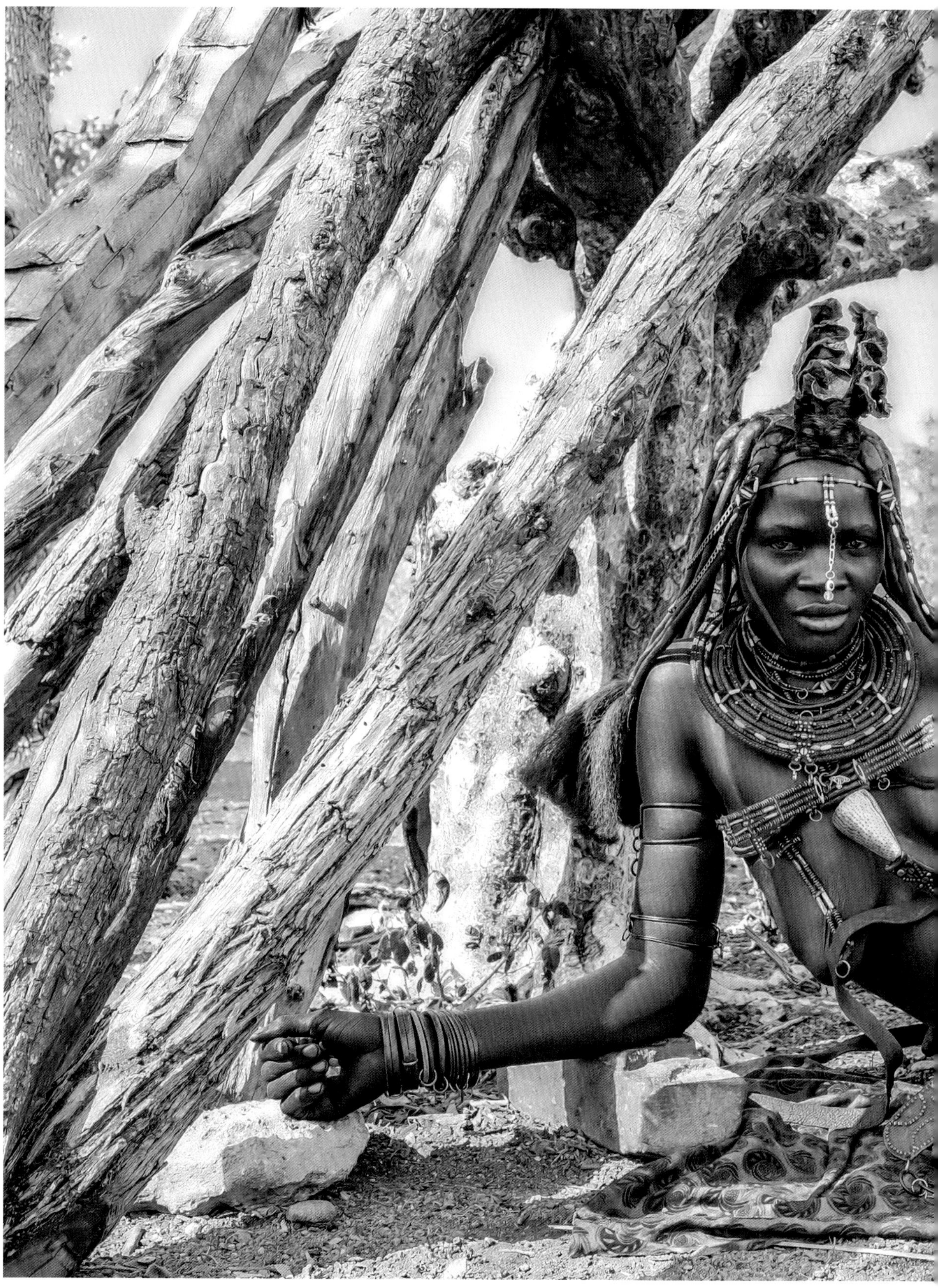

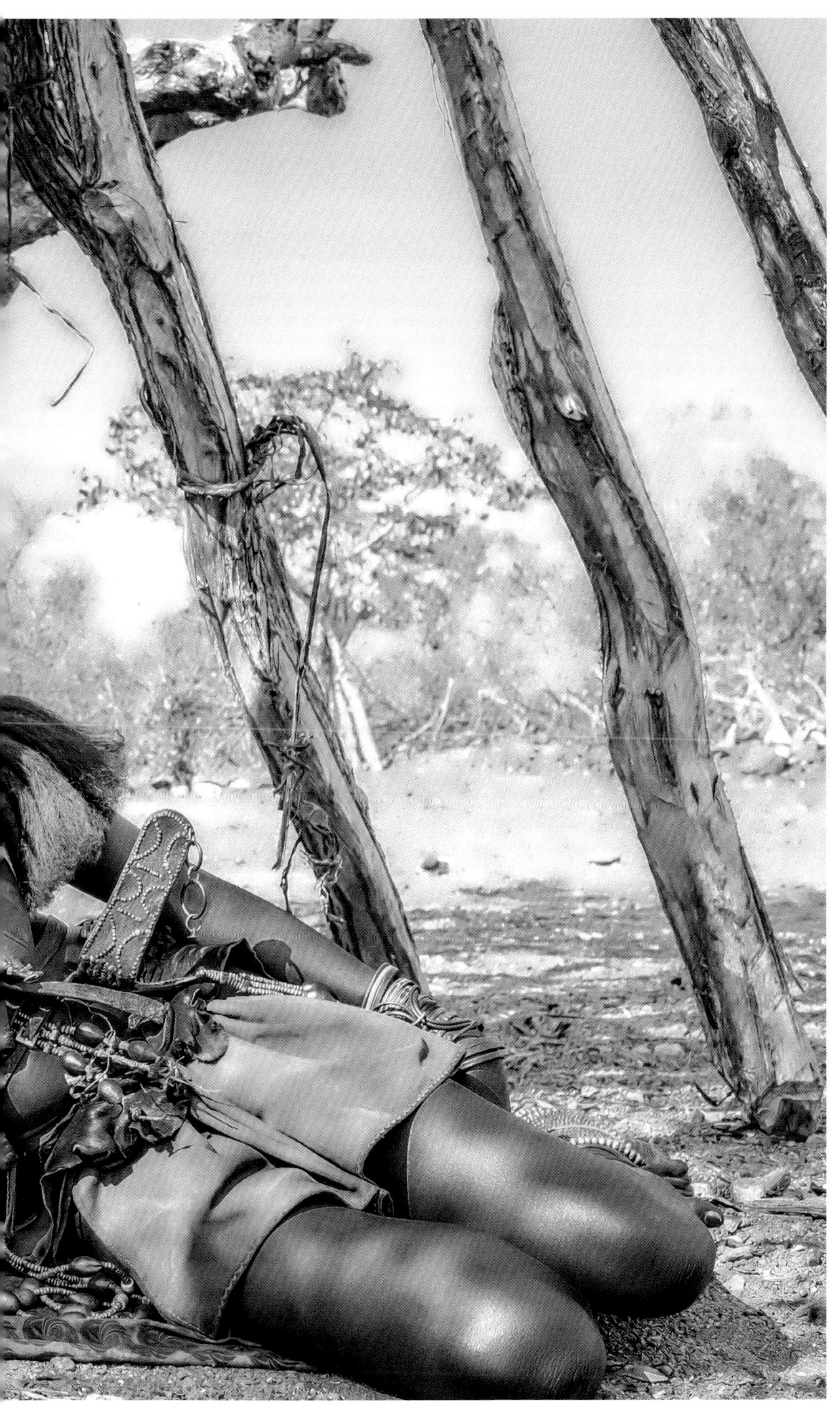

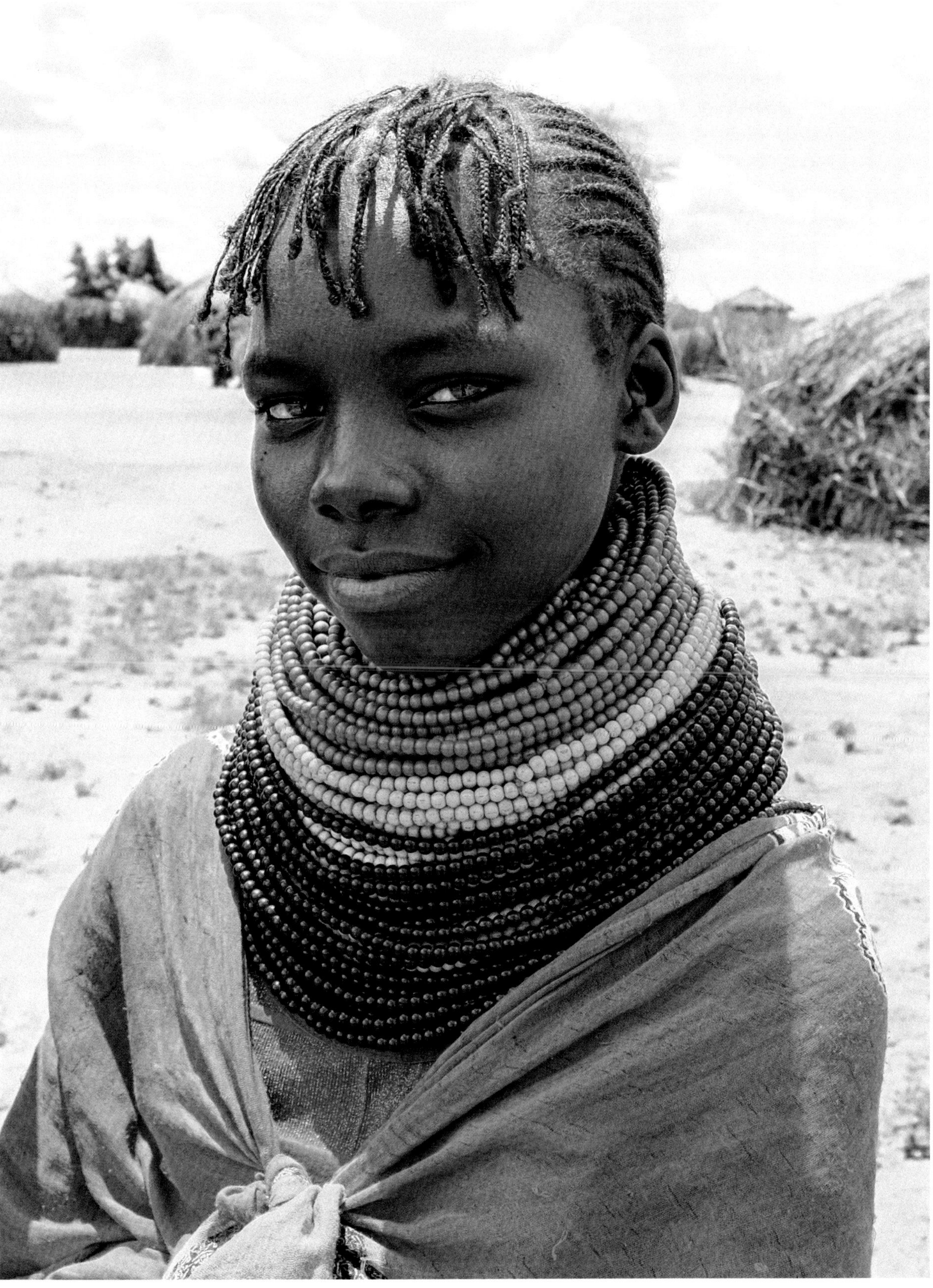

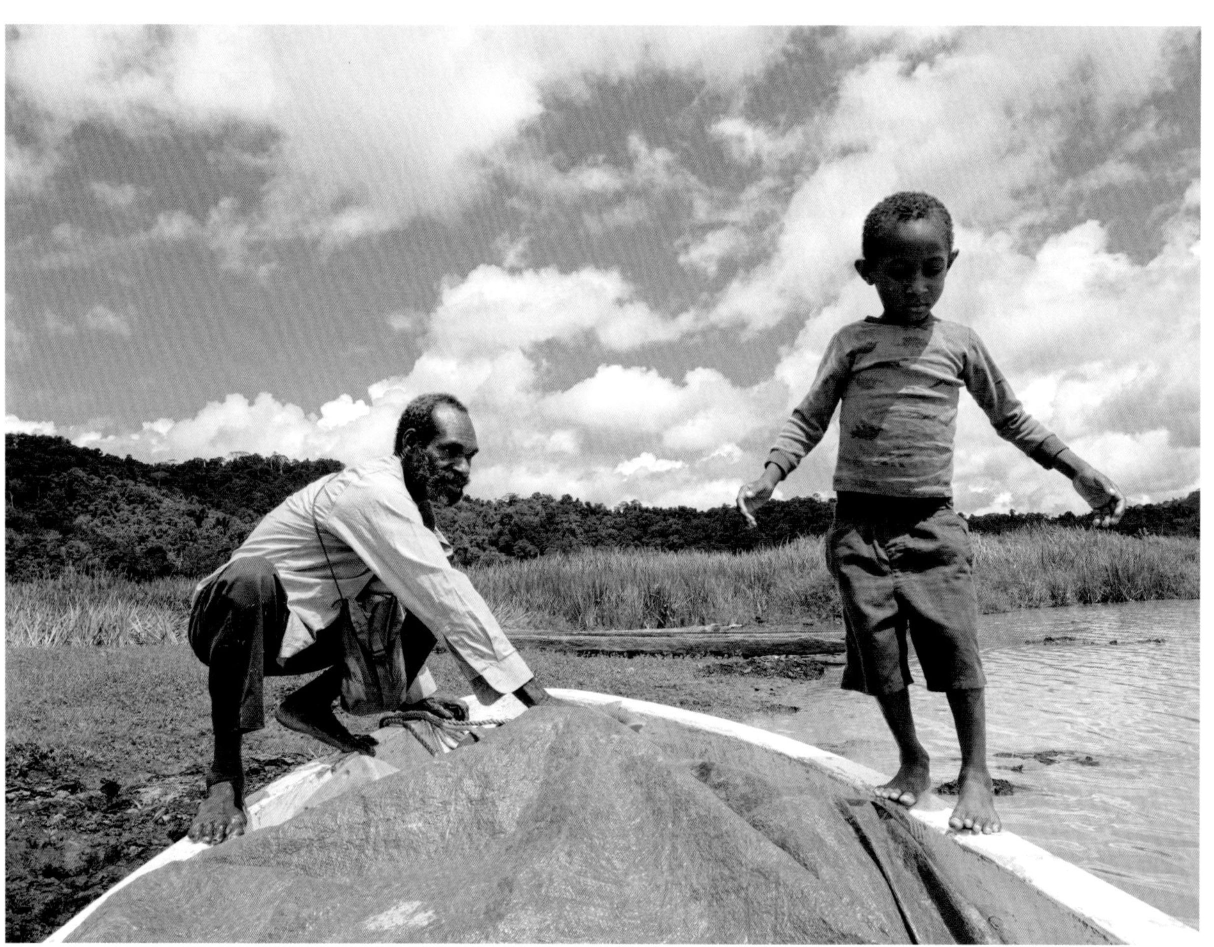

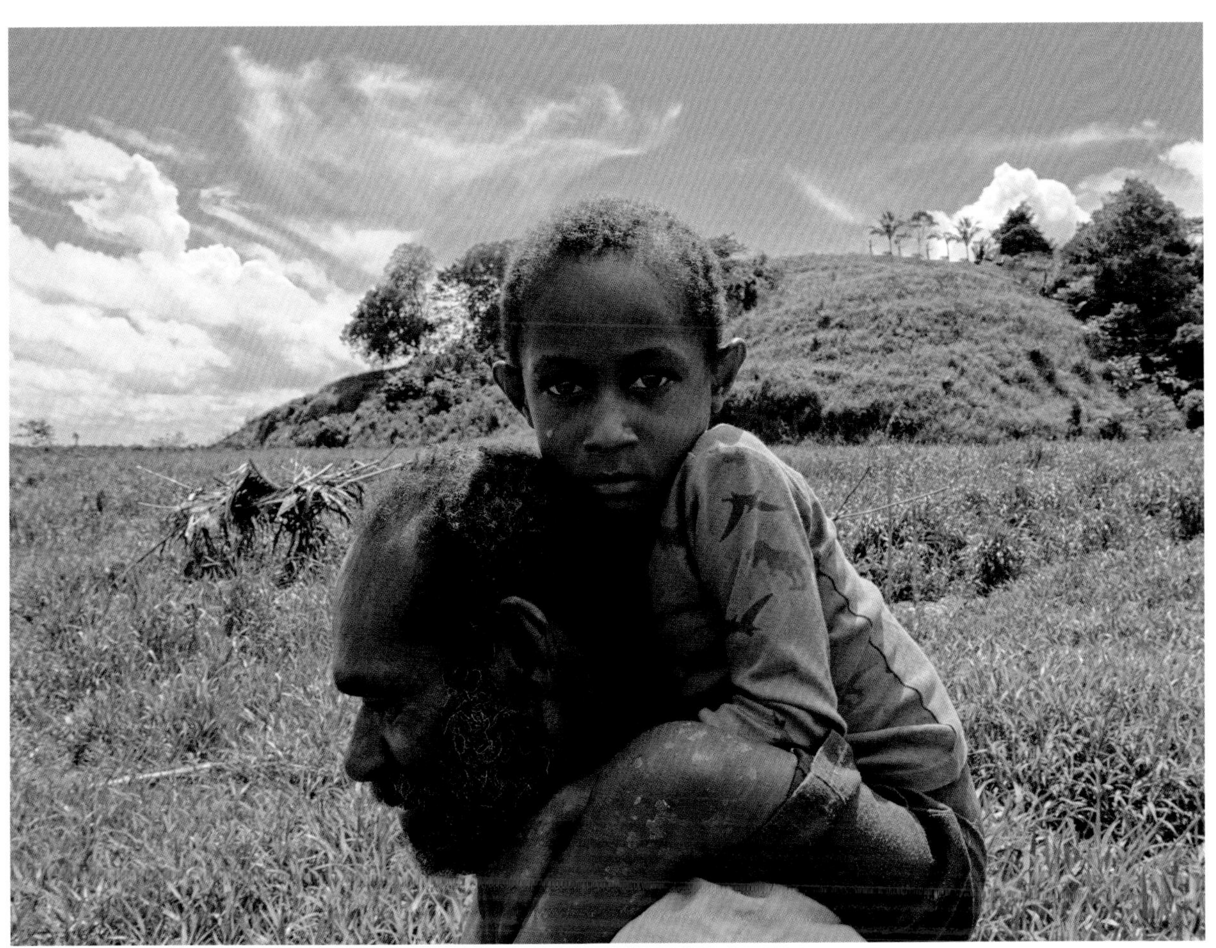

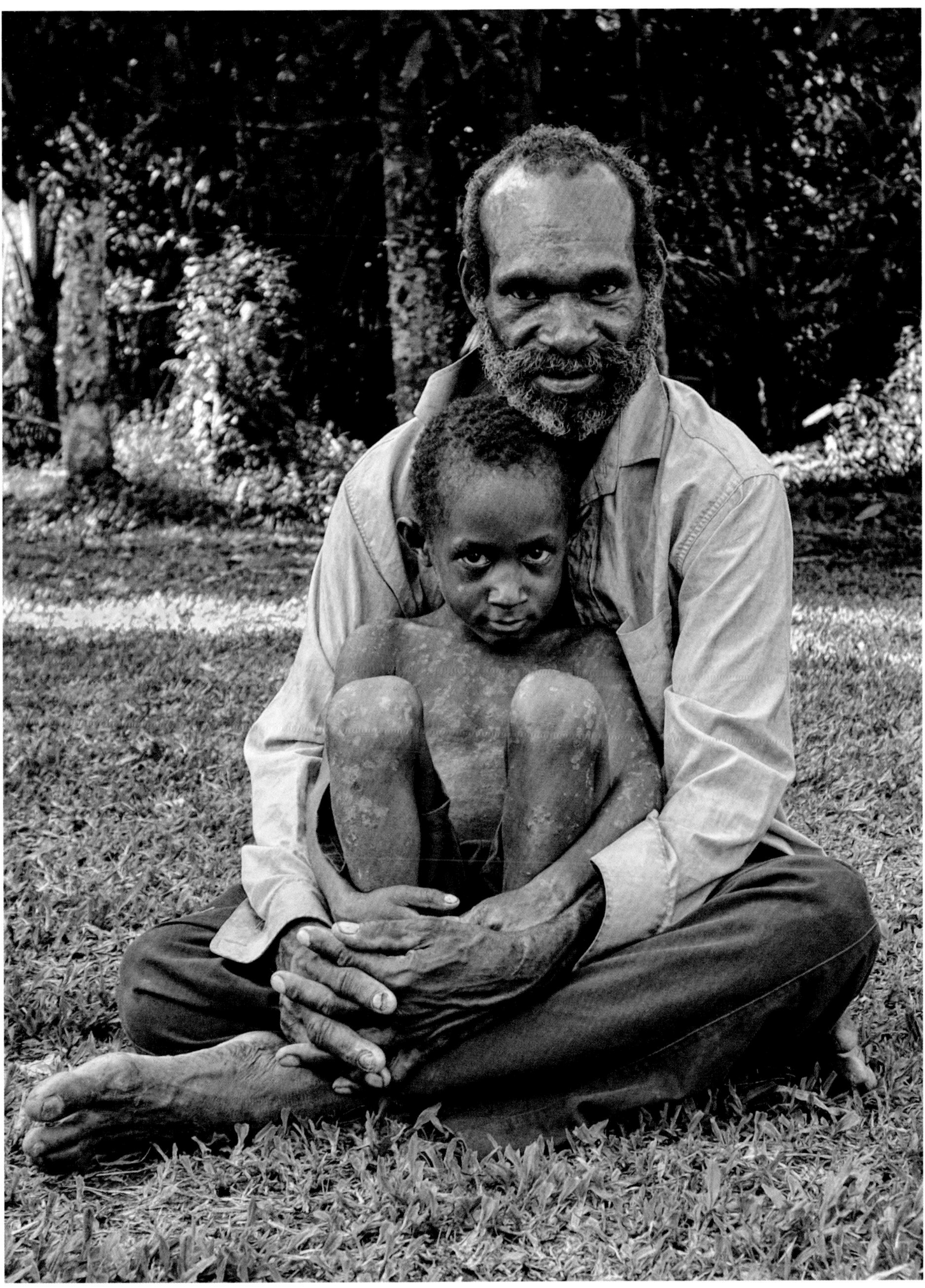

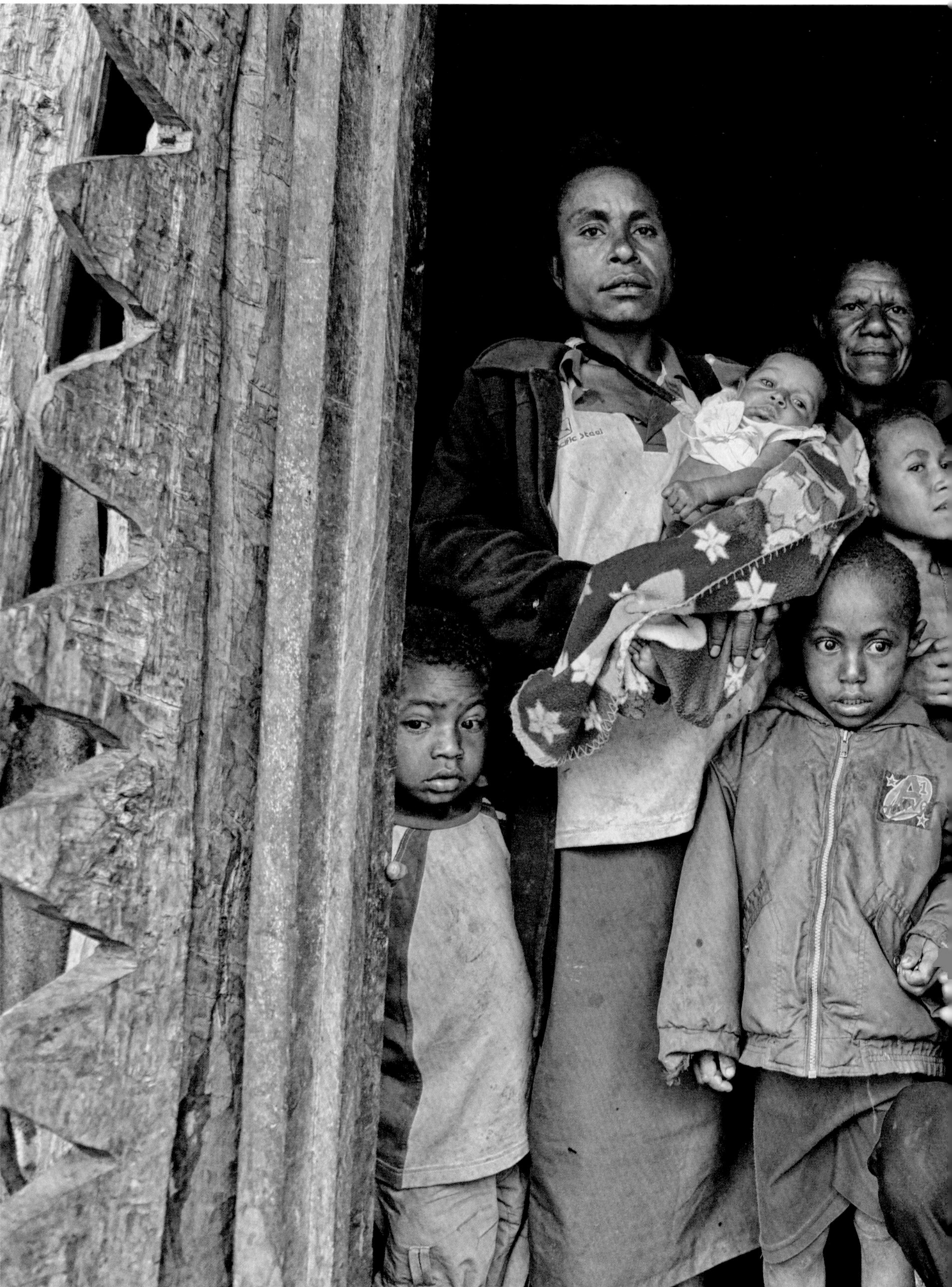

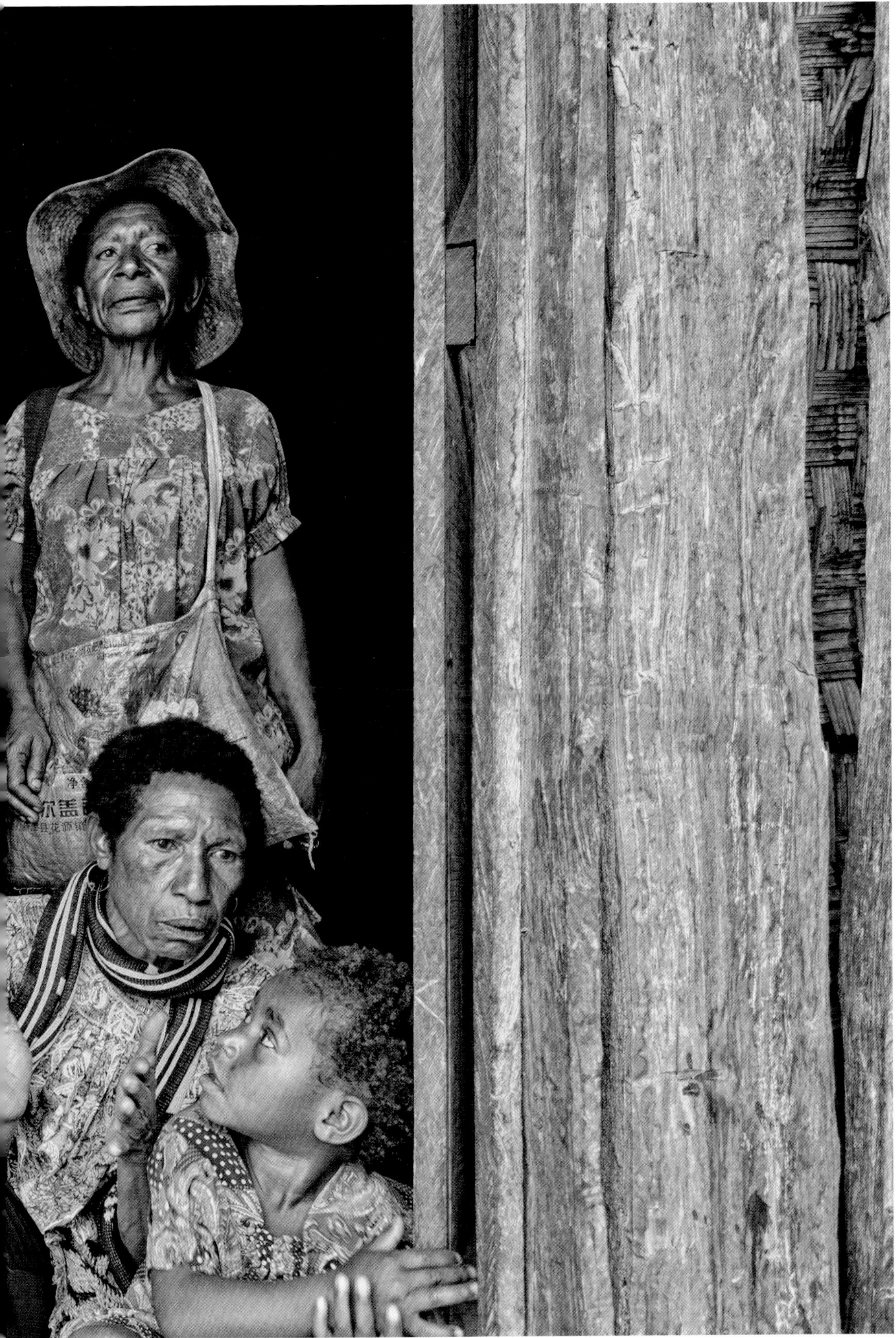

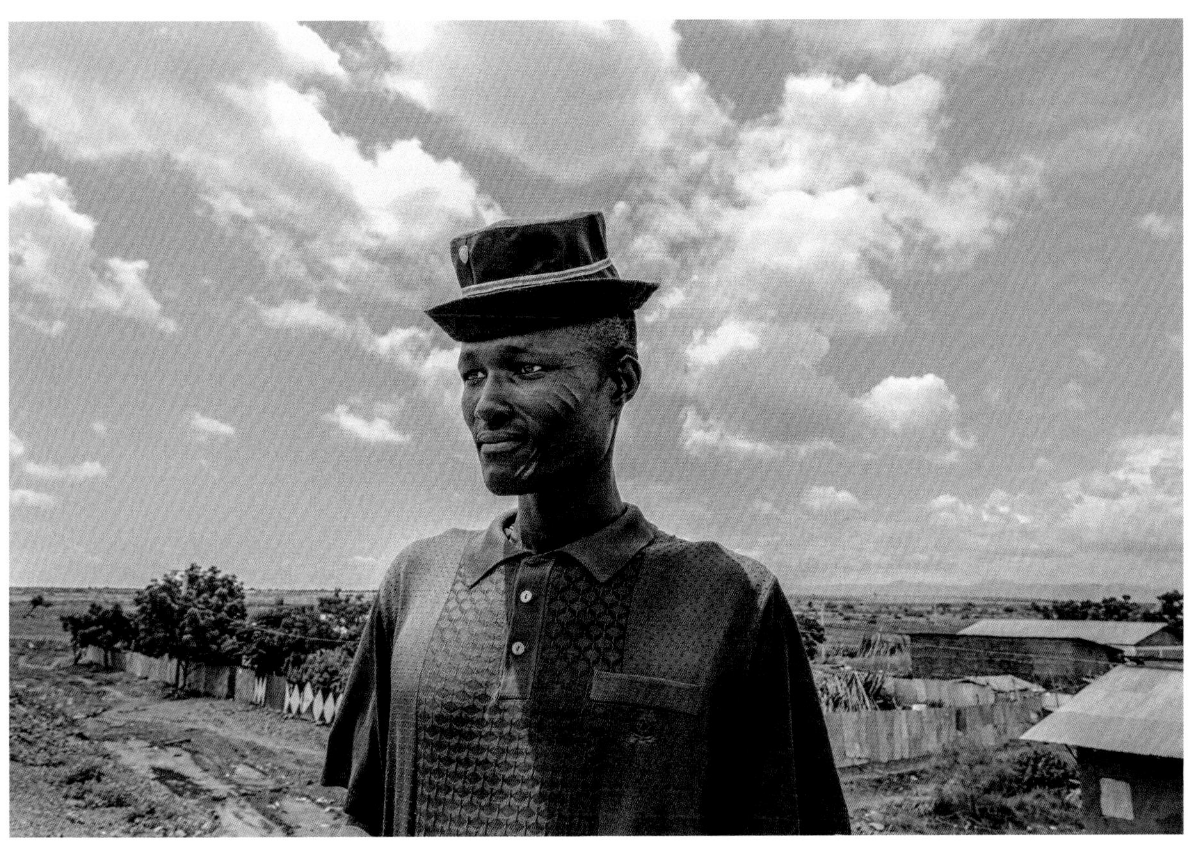

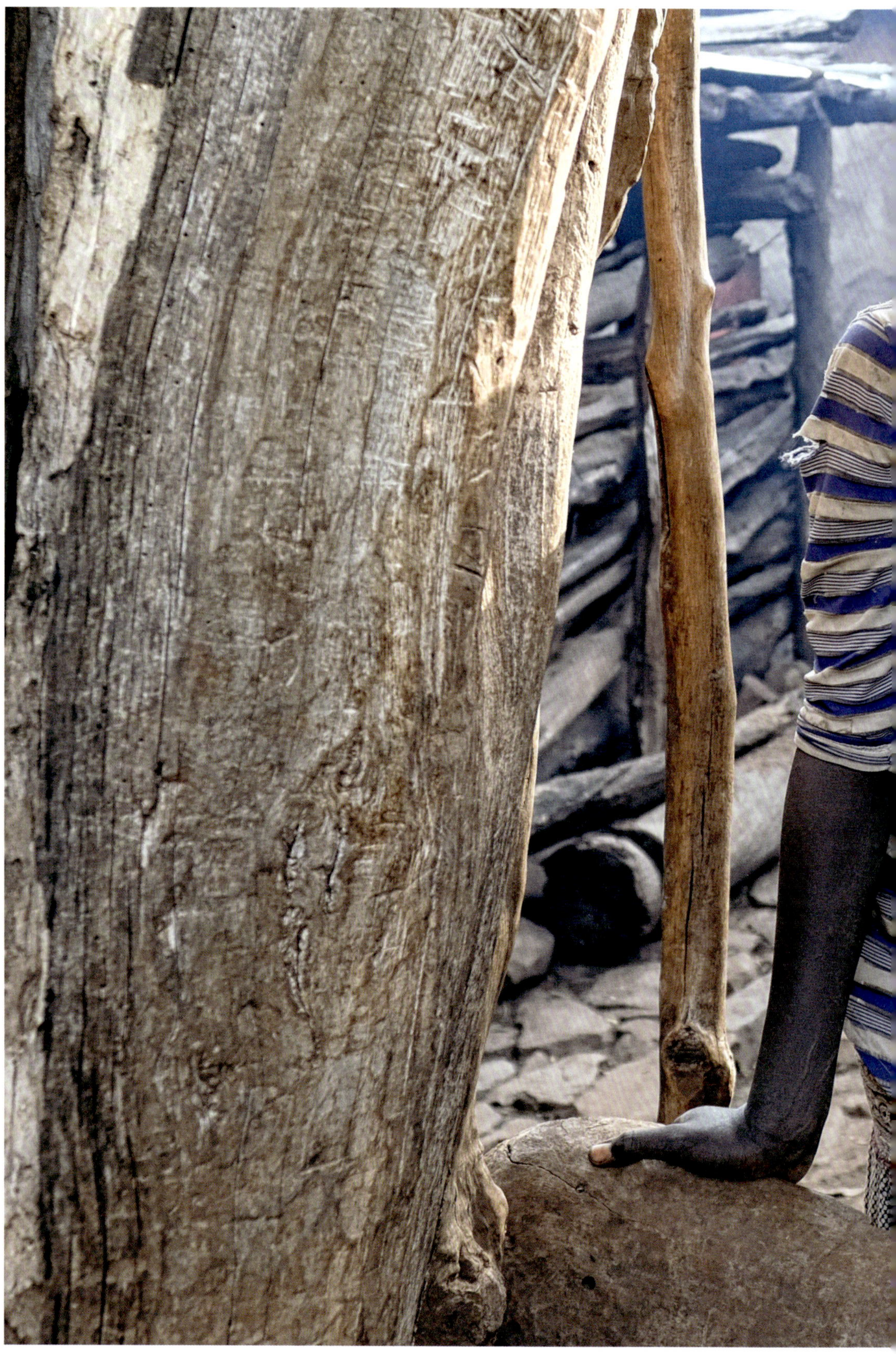

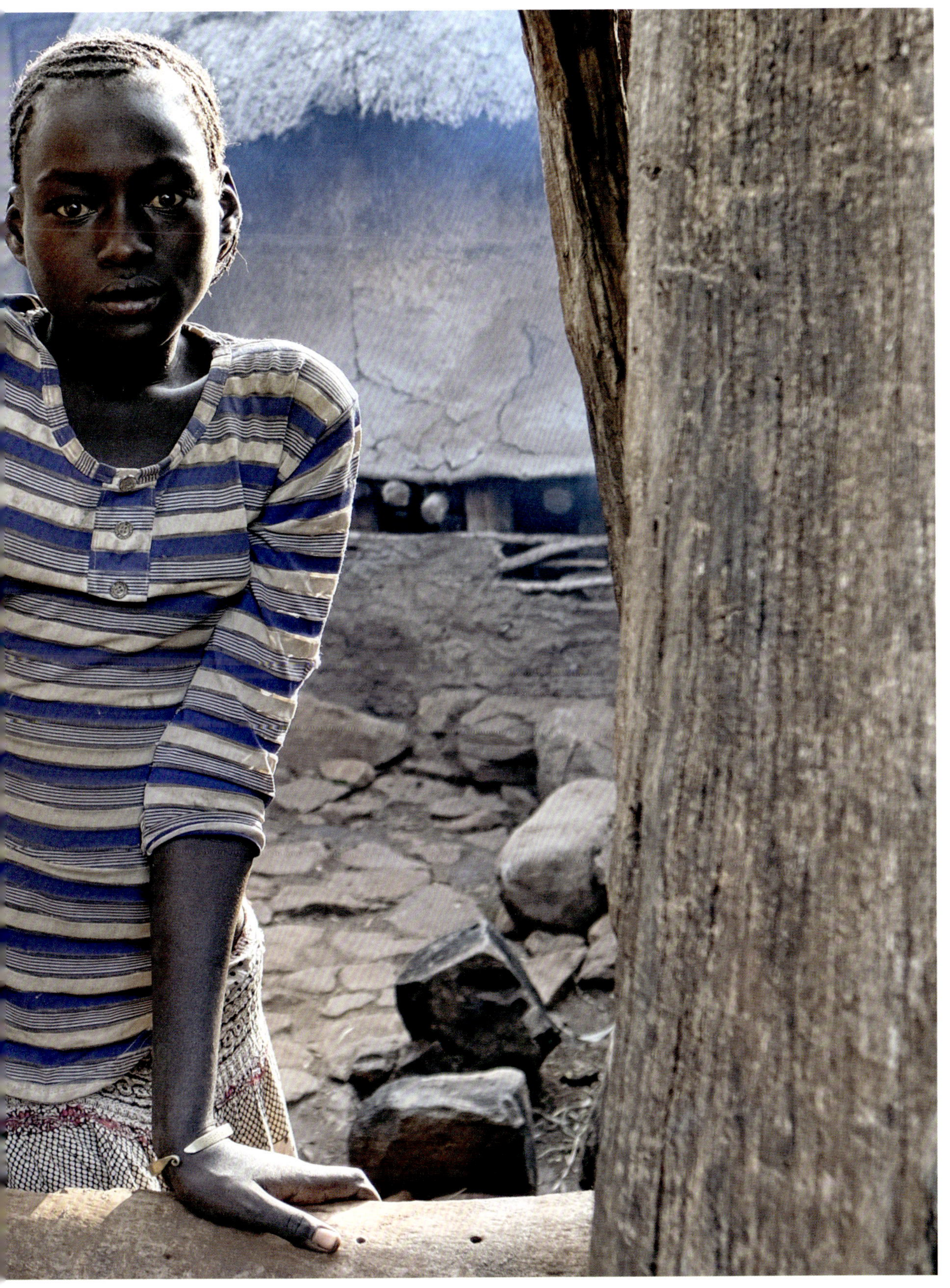

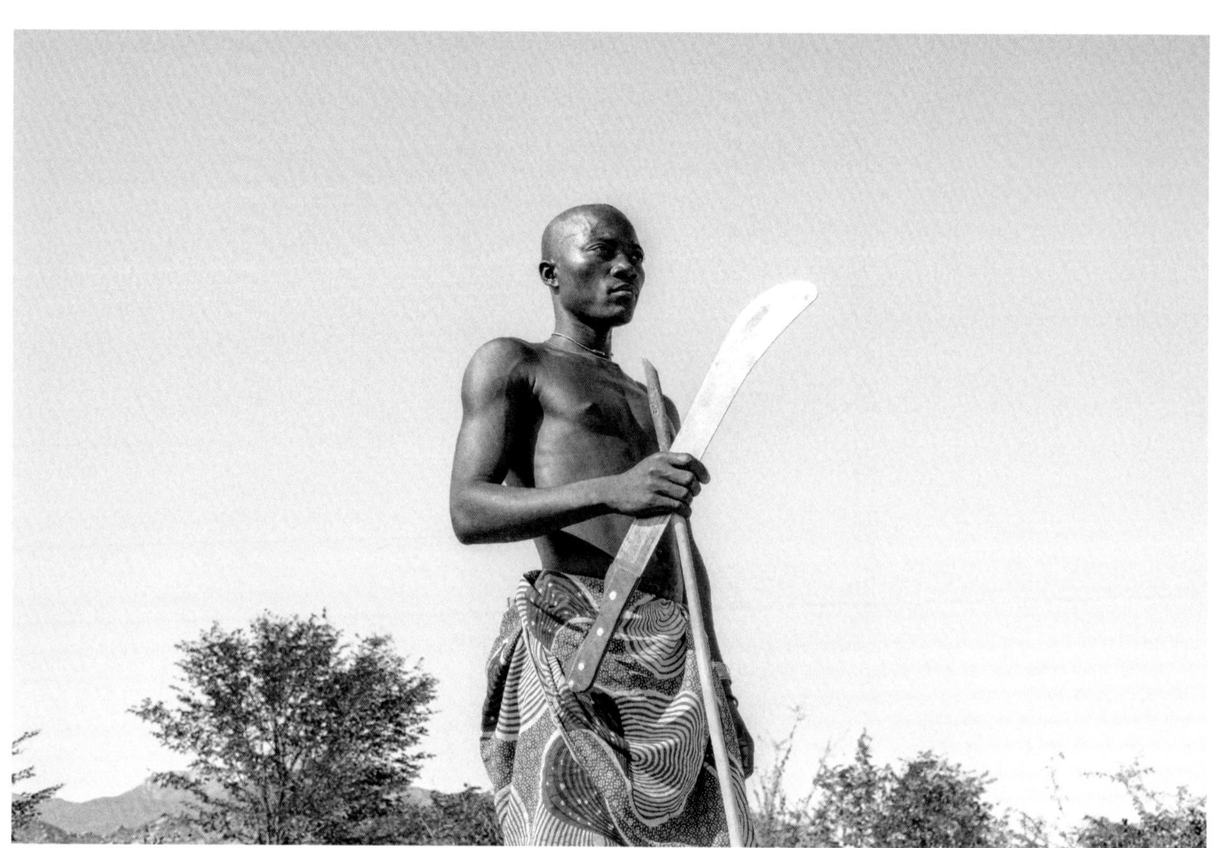

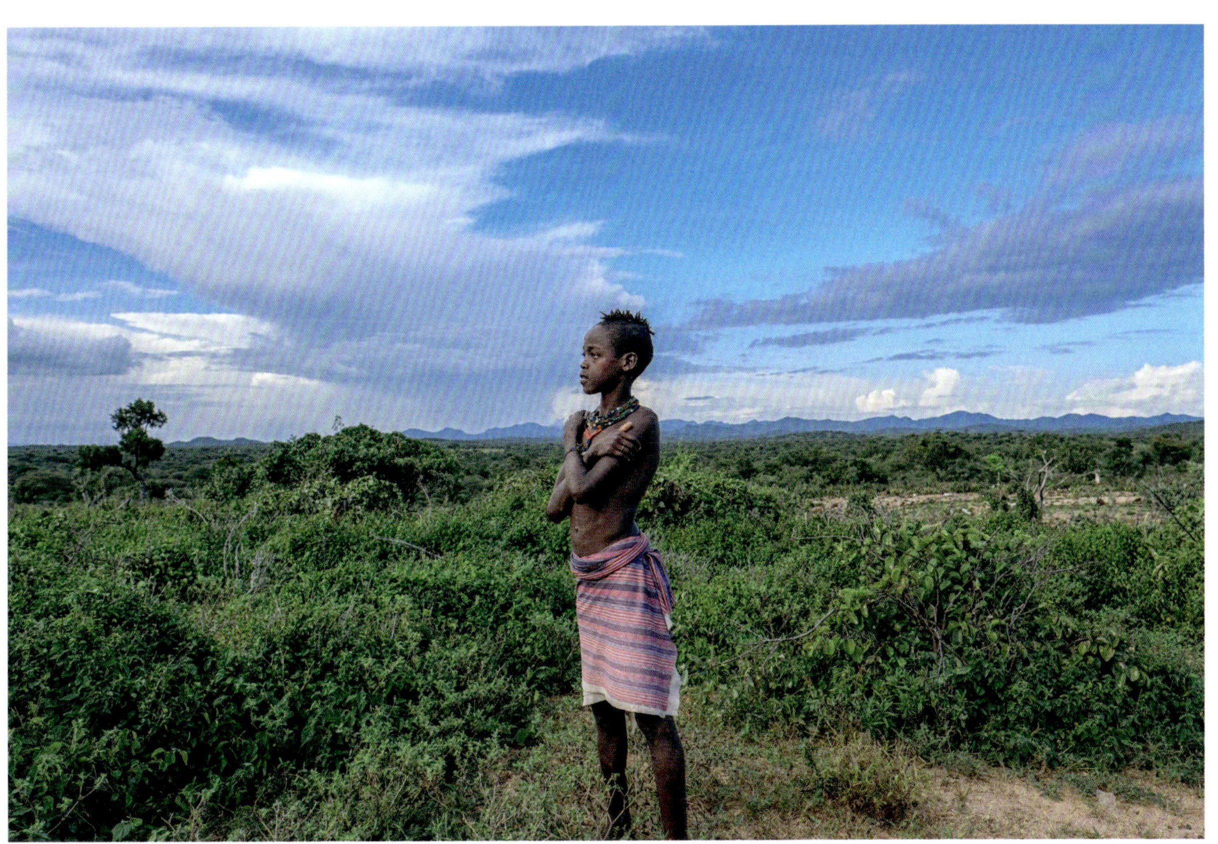

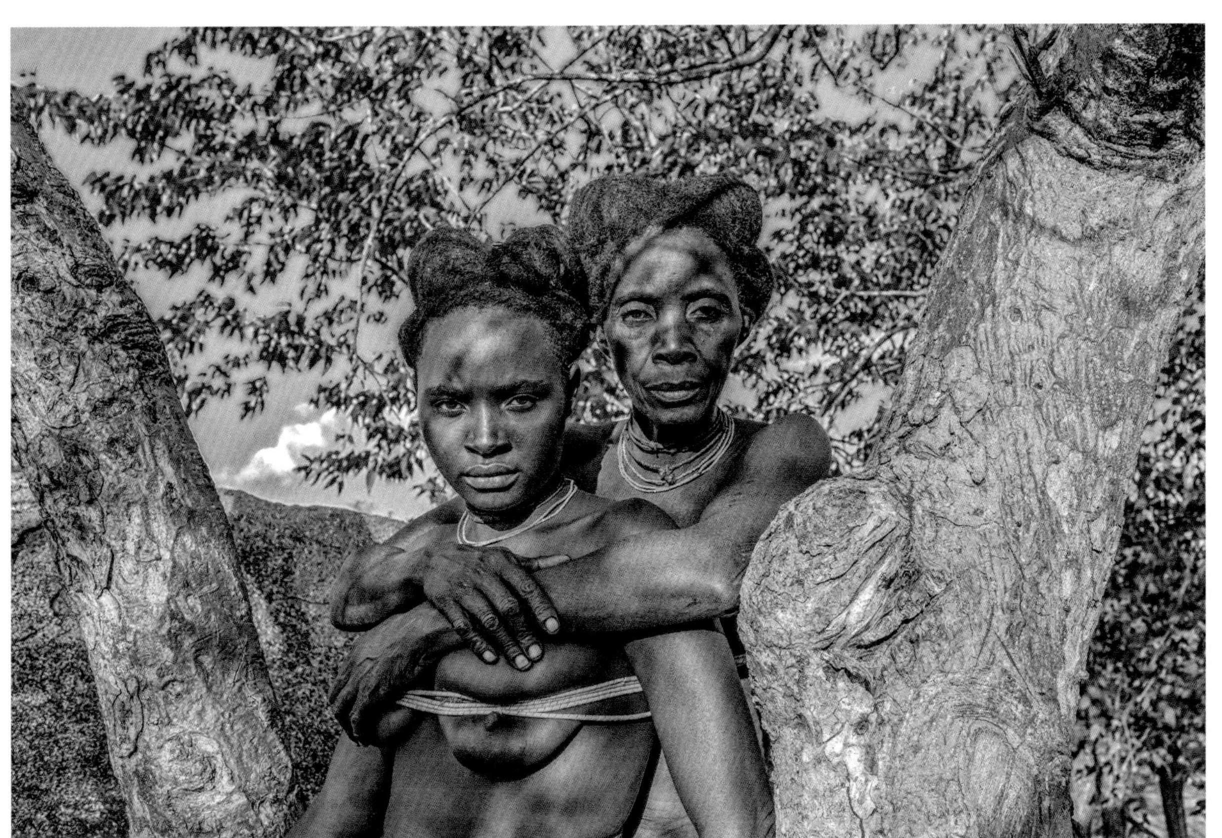

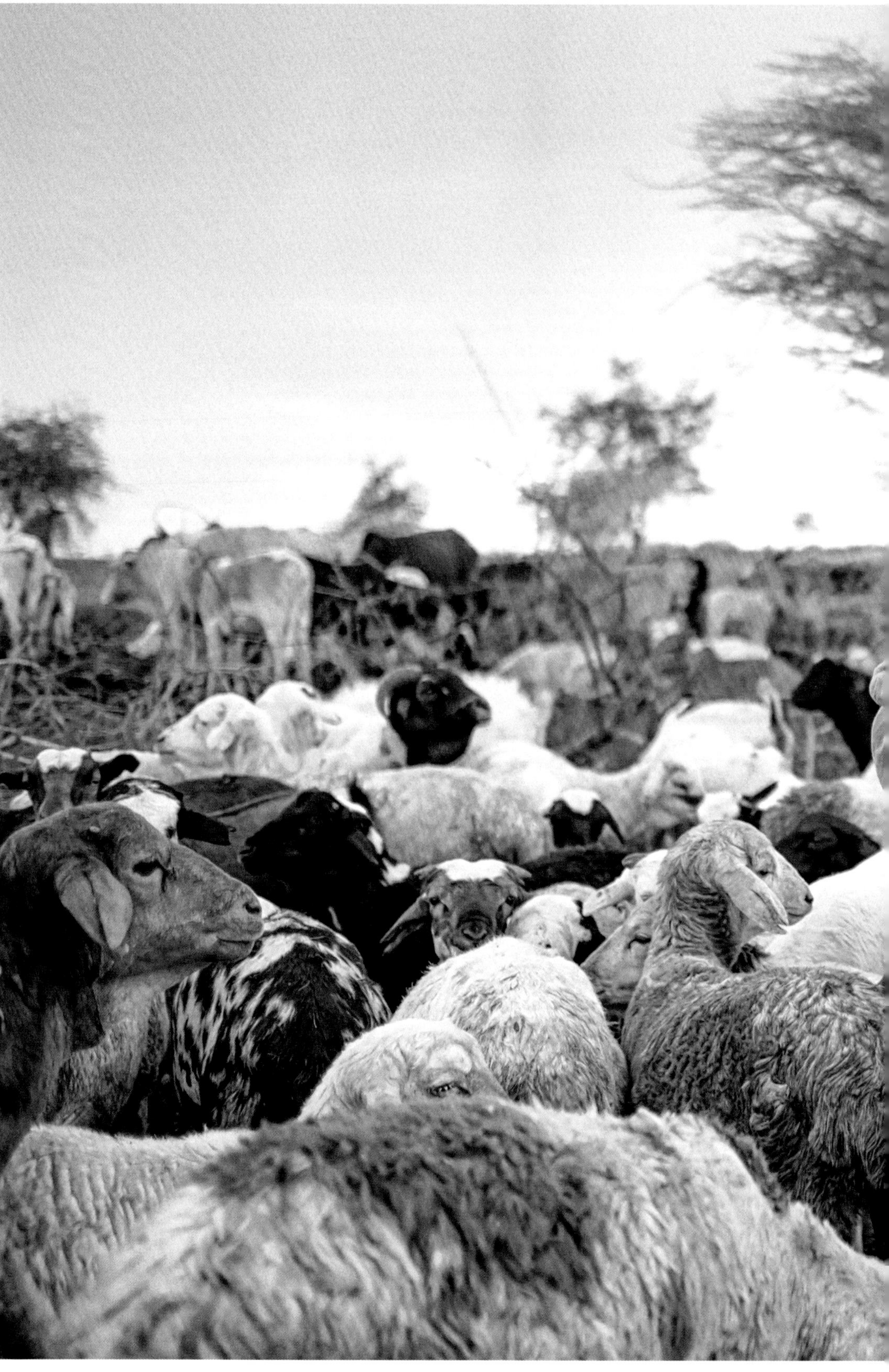

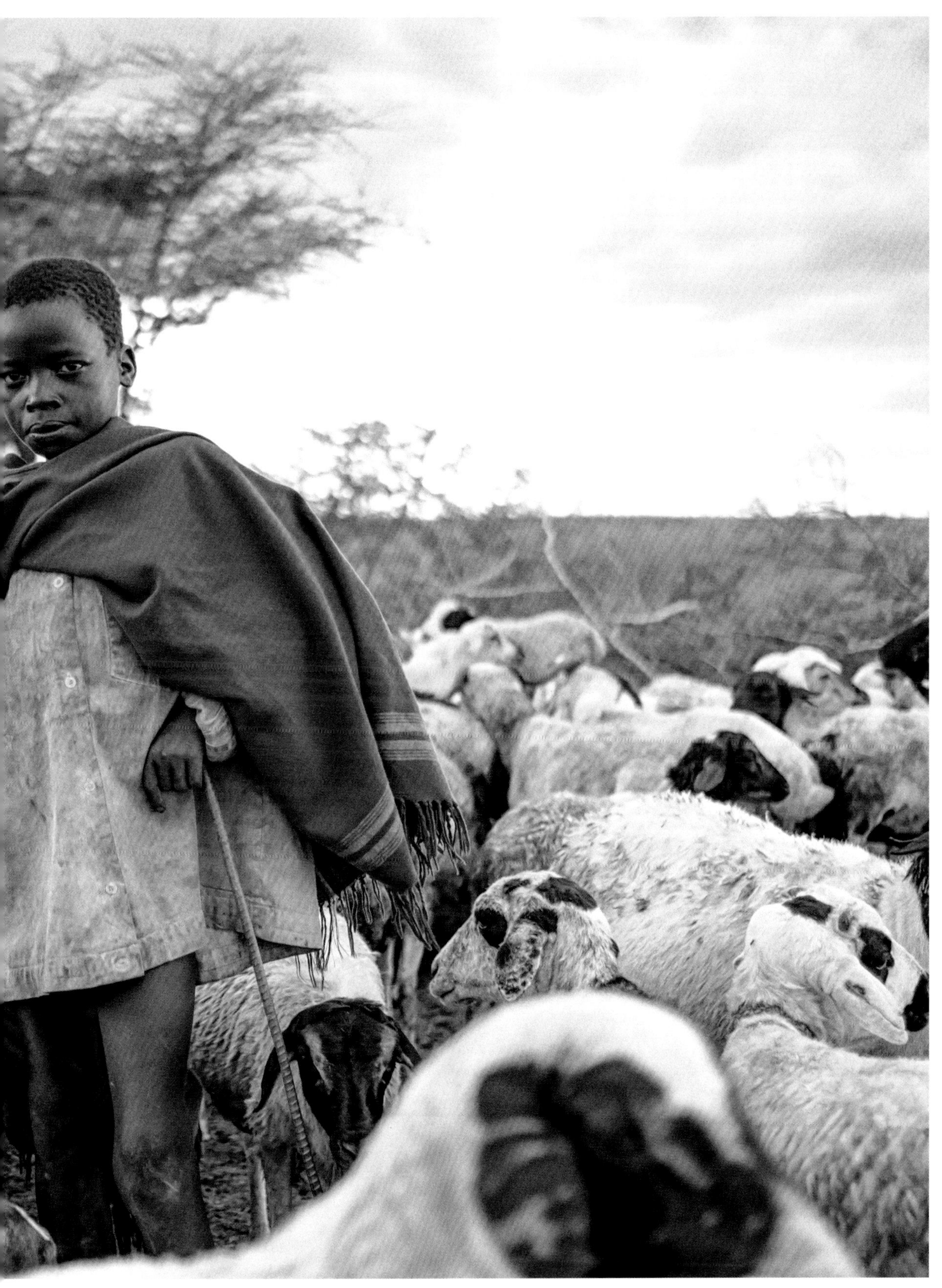

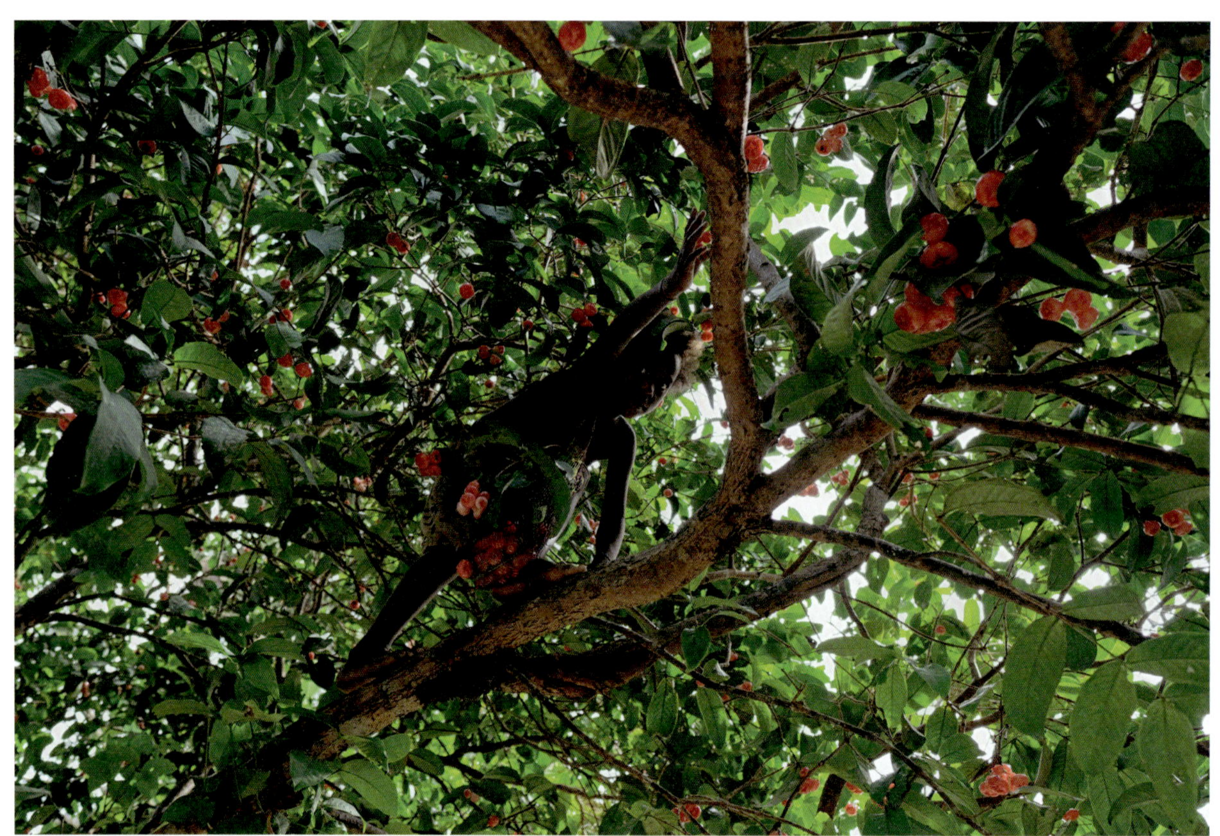

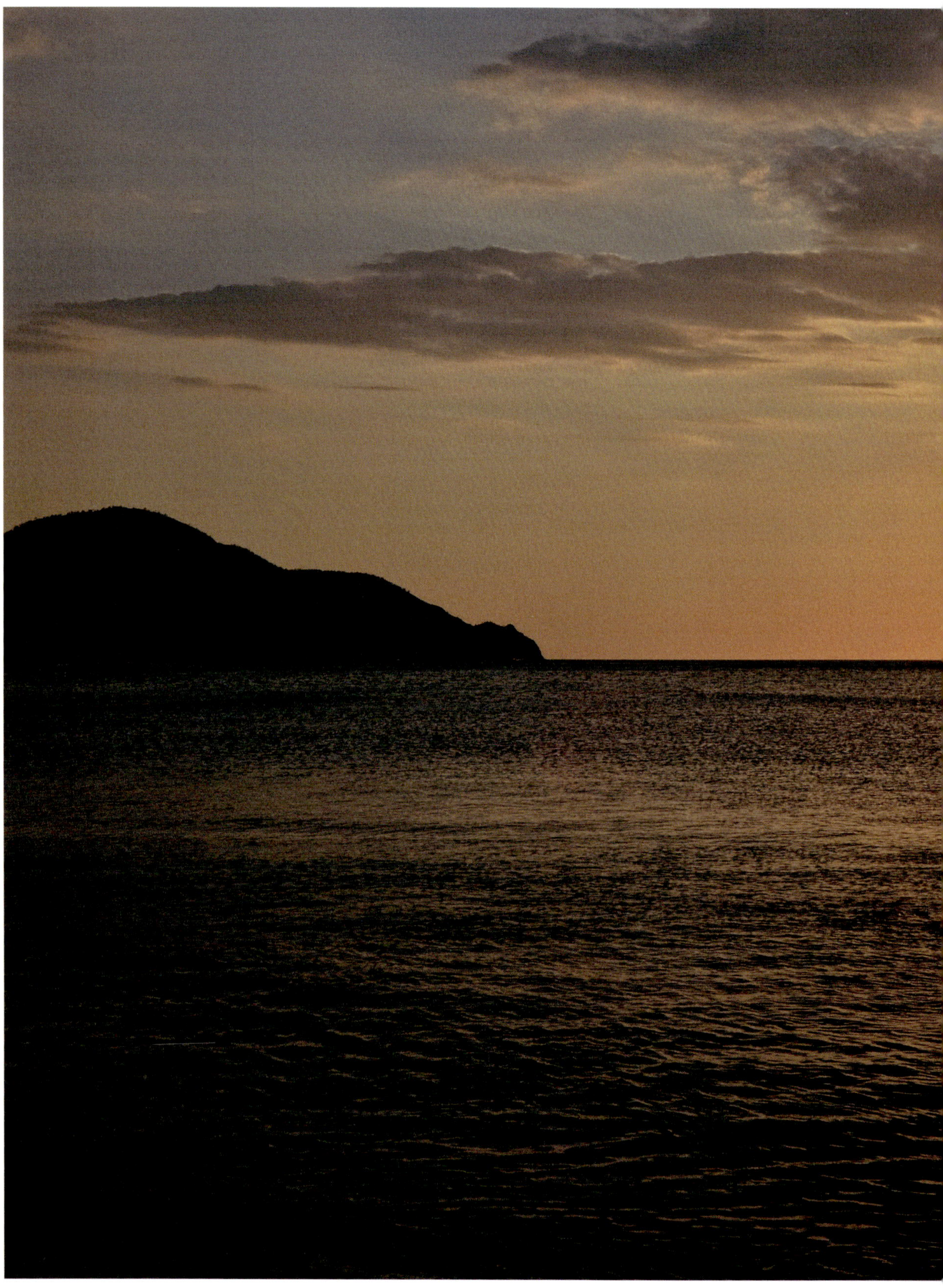

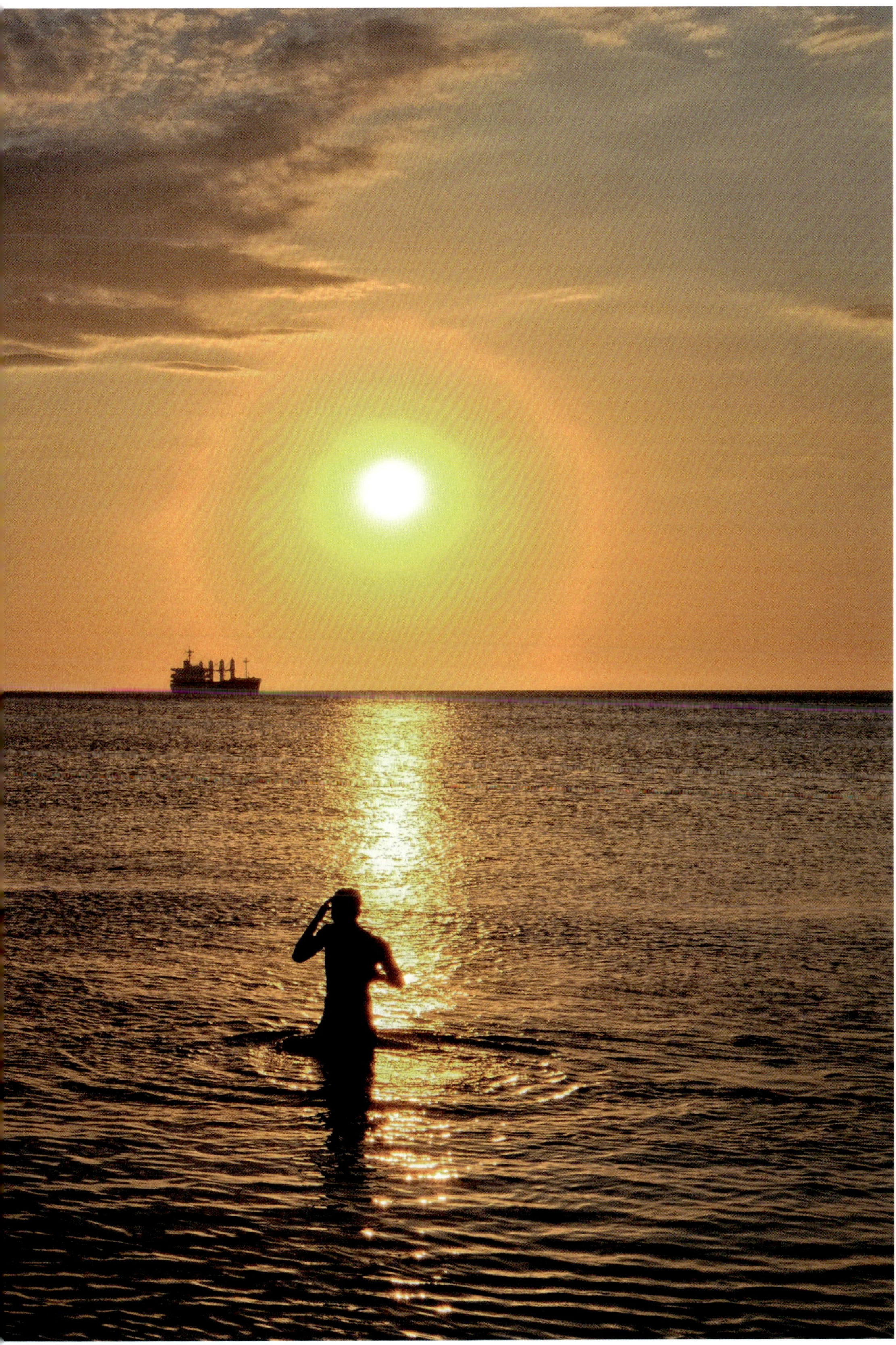

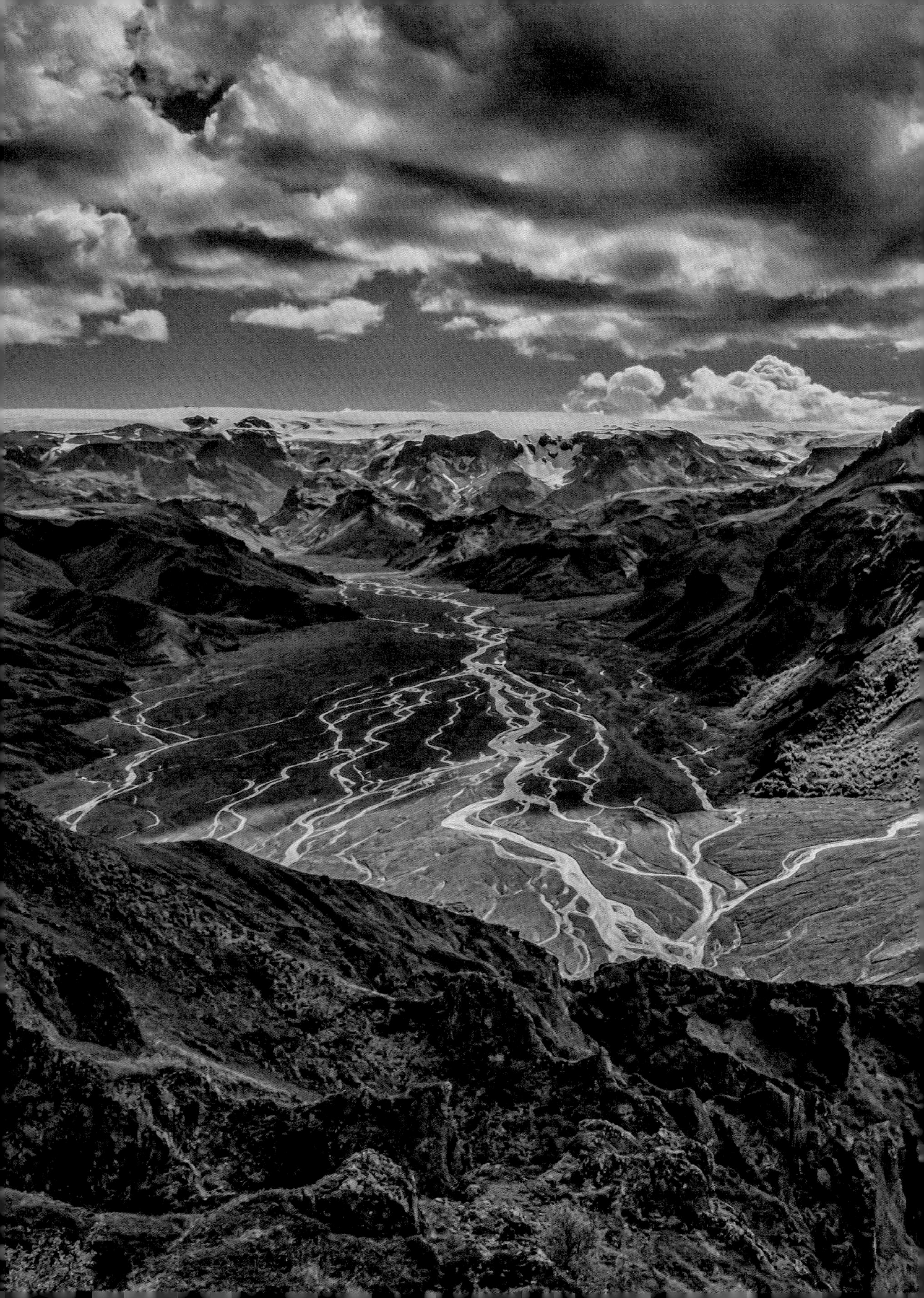

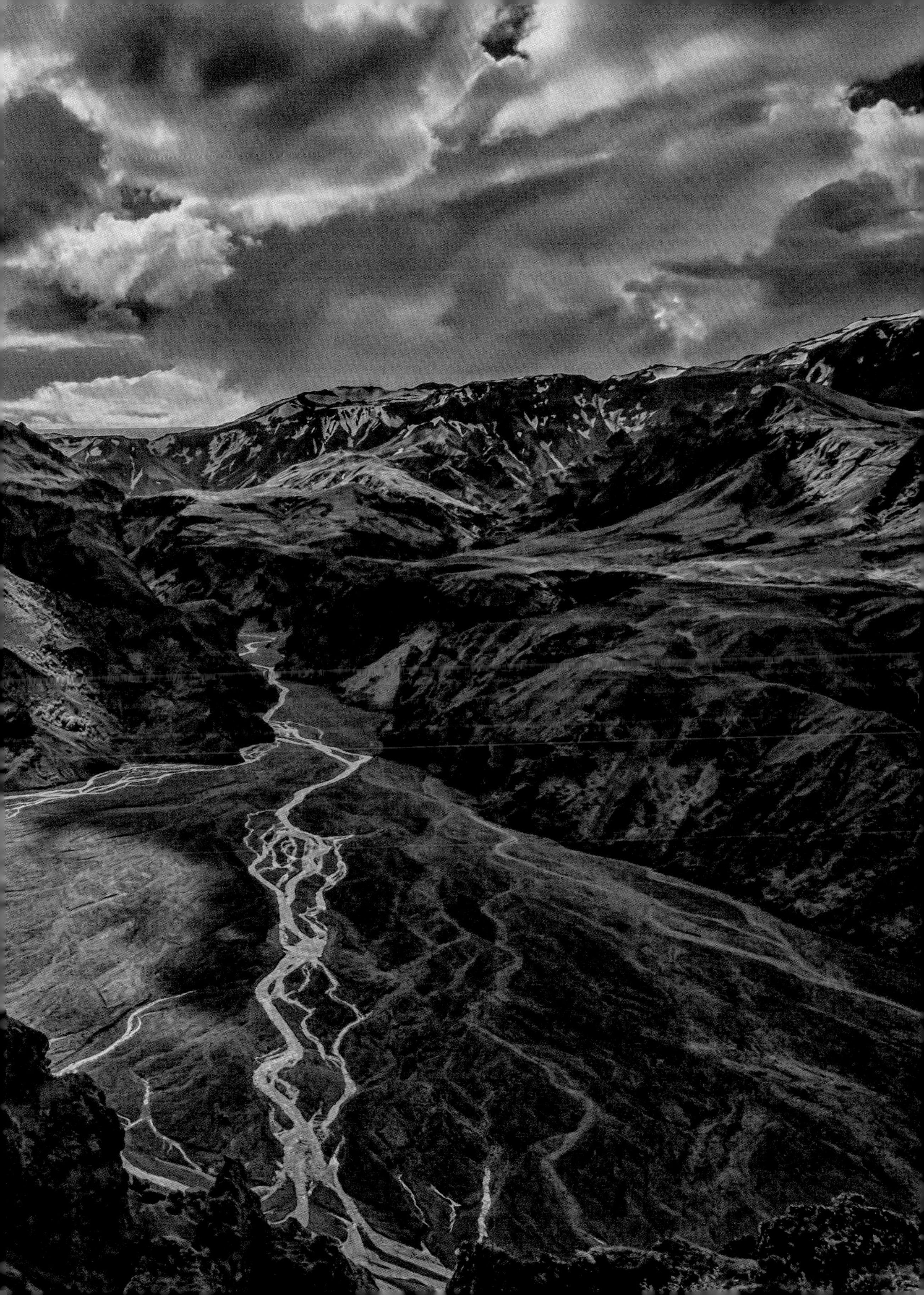

A SUM OF ONE

TREASURED MEMORIES

by Mike and Celia Hardiman

The natural world is full of amazing and spectacular treasures just waiting to be discovered. A photographer captures these treasures methodically, through a camera lens, and stores them to share with others. Celia and I capture them in our hearts. Both ways demand a spirit of curiosity, a willingness to face up to challenges, lots of patience, and the ability to develop an empathy with your surroundings.

Fortunately, like the image preserved by camera, the human brain connects with the heart doing much of the same with the finer details. All it takes is a little courage born from fate to make the leap and the rest is recorded history.

Celia and I first met for a few passing minutes in her sister's kitchen. Love at first sight? Certainly a connection. Time was kind to us and several months later we met again by chance, and the rest is our history in diaries kept.

These are a few select passages from our hearts.

August 15, 1996

• Our first sighting of the rings of Saturn on our first overseas camping adventure in Strathcona Provincial Park on Vancouver Island. Dark skies pinpricked with thousands of distant stars highlighting to us just how vast the universe is and how small we are. A humbling moment for us both.

January 6, 2020

• Hippos in Kenya viewed relaxing in the muddy river water below while we breakfasted together at the top of a steep bank which we hoped they hadn't yet learned to climb.

April 6, 2019

• Swimming as fast as we could to keep up with a massive whale shark off Ningaloo Reef, Australia, after its 4,000-km annual migration journey. A breathtaking experience over far too soon.

July 9, 2001

• Our first view of Machu Picchu from the Sun Gate. A great reward achieved by trekking on the Inca Trail via the frozen, snow-covered Dead Women's Pass. Teammates under a leaky tent on through altitude sickness, but all was worth it as we marveled at the ancientness in the valley below.

December 28, 2005

• Sliding down an icy slope near smelly penguins in Antarctica. Then shared pain with one of the parents when a skua swooped down and stole their chick.

February 24, 2015

• Sitting together on the top of Moreeb Dune. Sand stretching to the horizon on view. It's on the edge of the Empty Quarter, a vast uninhabitable region that challenges adventurers. We simply enjoyed an energetic morning's hike before returning to civilization.

October 27, 2020

- The view of the Reifhorn from Celia's mother's home in Lofer, Austria. A dramatic mountain peak covered in snow nearly all year round. This mountain has been the backdrop of many family gatherings and celebrations. A sight welcomed into by Celia's love.

Solo, neither of us had traveled very far, but together it was meant to be. All seven continents shared together. If it's an image, a quote, a meeting in a kitchen that captures your imagination, our advice is just go with the serendipity, and you too will be in a place of love.

Stephanie Parsons,
You saw me
In a particular way
Believed in my work
Connected me to Daylight
Thank you
I love you
Ever yours

—DS

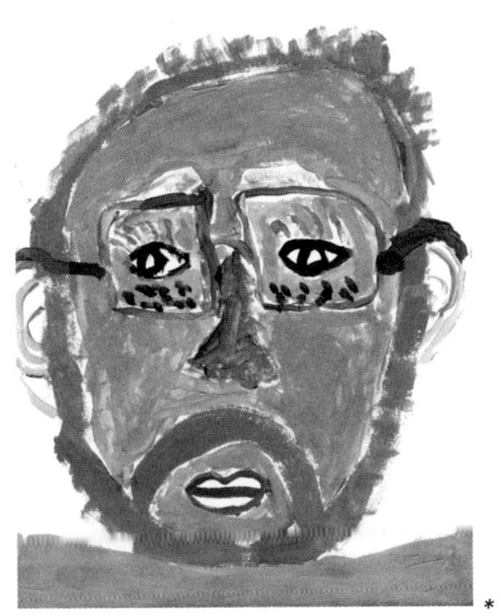

*drawing by Ava Jacobson

JOURNAL

13/06/16

Once there was no desire to travel. Then I went to the beat of my own drum inside me of which grew loud(er). I walked to that beat. I went plenty of places. Enough to stoke satisfaction. Never would I ~~would~~ go here. Until I flipped over a found WWII photograph of my Opa and read "New Guinea Glenn E. Schrock Feb 1945". Flash ahead and now I'm sitting outside on a grass strip waiting to hitchhike to a Mission Aviation Fellowship Cessna in the high mountains of Papua New Guinea to avoid what I understand is a violent situation on the mountain road. To think someone took it upon themselves to warn a stranger. Kindly advise them otherwise is a remarkable gesture. It's difficult to hear this news of strife remembering the faces I saw when I crammed into a public motor van and complete strangers on their own journeys in their own lives made room for me. Freed a seat from seeds and stock, cleaned it, and shook my hand, welcoming me. Spoke to me as they would a new neighbor. Breaking a banana in two. I've come to learn the world is kind and severe and oftentimes in the same place. Difficult, though necessary to understand. Perhaps the severity strengthens the kindness. ~~[crossed out]~~ I've encountered the kind so overwhelmingly the reasons for travel were a blessing, as is ~~[crossed out]~~ the road. I see no inconvenience waiting for a flight that may or may not come. These moments are on the wings of others. I trust them. And much of traveling is in the wait. Waiting for a flight. A train. A pot to boil. A rain to pass. A dream to form. An inspiration. A sign to go. I had my Opa! So thank you to whoever took Negative Number NWS 32 for the American Red Cross, you documented 2 generations.

Glenn Schrock

Colombia Feb '17

Under ~~shadows~~ shadows of a Lost City.
Vines fall from infinity. The immediacy
of the jungle is to love. A great romance.
A score of nature. Stimuli to the eye.
Traveling light. Species surround my
ignorance, to walk on my skin, upon
my flesh. I have ~~not~~ acquired a
synchronizing breath with nature as
I am taken.

Ciudad Perdida

Kanazawa   June 6, 2018

Mayumi. Her and I sat at the bar of a
Japanese steakhouse. We met at lunch, a
sushi bar. By the sharing of food. Her
workday ended. I had an afternoon walk.
Late night dining. Much of the city seems
asleep. Though amazingly lit. Bar tended
by a master and a much younger sous-
chef. ▓▓▓ Glow of intermittent street
lights hit and miss. Us two, the only
customers. Yakiton. Grilled vegetables. Rice.
Beer. Conversationally, she spoke no English.
I joked in dry humor, said I would
teach her. I spoke no Japanese. Yet I
learned over a meal of her business
career, ballet lessons, learning to draw
and color - and seeing some of her work,
where she was from and her family.
She ordered our dishes with my trust.
She asked of me. All of this on
google translate. I spoke of the trip

I was on from Ethiopia → Japan. Why such different places to pick to travel and showed the map of routes, in total will circle the world. She asked if I photograph and what I use - A retro style Fuji, rectangular, just as we see. My preference for Japanese minimalism in the arrangement of lines. Oma and Opa to their grandchildren. The United States. American ballgames - movies! The wilderness and being soft-spoken. To tell one person I will never see again just exactly what I'm chasing and what it means. I think she understood the arrangement of my lines, and the soft-spokenness didn't exist in the between.

In translation

May 24, 2018

Pitched a tent in a goat enclosure of a village belonging to the Hamer. A boy gave me a hand, about a decade younger. I needed the hand to survive. Semi-desert land to mountains stacked in the horizon. Southern Ethiopia. He wasn't traditional. Modern, I suspect from his motorbike trips from the village to surrounding towns. Sunglasses. Adidas. A fair amount of bling. He wore the bracelet of his ████ tribe. Tying himself to his mother - fully traditional. Hair of buttered red soil and a collar around her neck. Though his father, much like him. The father and I shared beer. The son and I shared a conversation - about a sense of home and place. He has no desire to leave his village in Ethiopia for anywhere else in the world. Not a plane ticket to anywhere. The American Dream has no pull here. It doesn't translate.

Home is home and culture runs thick. His village, his culture lives handed down from the past. Despite not being of the traditional sense, he's culturally woven from the blood of his mother to his own beliefs agreed to as a young man. A life he chose and where he chose to have it. Not me, not money, not fame, not that ticket, not anything but here can penetrate his soul. He is as he is and his one preference is his land, familiarity, culture. In the evening, under its shade, he took off on a motorbike. Kicking dirt across a landscape. Faster and faster he went. I could see it, what he was talking about.

Motorbike

Sepik River Day 6 2017

Village to village. Canoeing the Sepik, upriver on the soul. No falsity of itinerary. A true sentence. Of hello's and goodbye's. Handshakes and shared waterfalls. My expedition, pushing off from a mud bank. Mud between the toes, I am in it. Never would have thought my nature would have the courage to do this, but here I am in this nature. Far and away, sailing into the jungles of myself. Of this landscape. Harsh. Hot. Wild. Hungry. The jungle is hungry and so I have traveled into it. Free to think, to be as much as I can bear. Something I've never contemplated before from the tears and cry of a boy. He was wide-eyed, crying, and reaching for his mother. What happened? He saw me! And? He had never seen a white man before. I had arrived as a ghost. Not a place, not in print, nor his imagination had he seen one. I stood in front of him, his sibling, his mother. The weight I felt. The privilege was immense. This was a responsibility of travel. Being a beginning. A beginning settled and his tears dried. His voice pronounced softly. The same boy once afraid relaxed into leaning next to me on the floor of his tree stilted house and smiled when he touched my eye. He was my last look when I pushed off from the riverbank.

white man

11-June-2012

Hiking these parts reclaims the ~~the~~ essence.
In the becoming smaller, to a speck of
hardened proportions, among these mountains
and glaciers and valleys. Under the ~~them~~
pressure of nature is the shaping of my
nature. Out of my way. Out of my head.
Out of the ego. Burying expectations.
Burying noise. ~~xxxxxxxxxxxxxxxxxxx~~
The wonder of the obstacle is the
point to seek.

Zermatt

Arba Minch
Ethiopia 2018

I love these streets! The bustle. Spray of traffic, dust, spices, noise. How people make eye contact. Acknowledge one another's presence. Ethiopian to Ethiopian. Modern to traditional... to a stranger's journey. I am not alone here. Not at all. Even in the chilliness of the south. Nights and early mornings. A cold shower starts the day to layers of dress I can shed. Out the door and around a corner to a coffee tent. Populated by a cool 20's generation. It's the spot, a local Central Perk. I am a passive one, not to push myself upon anyone, as all the ~~seating~~ seating seemed taken. I had no expectations of a scoot left, scoot right for me. I have no entitlement. But, the coffee drinkers saw me. That I could use a hot cup, and a pair split apart and the rest squeezed a little tighter. Tighter yet, when I squeezed in. The pouring of coffee in Ethiopia is an art. The steam we share, words spoken in its breath. The perfect shade of black falls like a waterfall in Geirangerfjord from a silver kettle and the sound it makes hitting the stained glass cup is the mechanics of time. A perfect sound to meet the moment. A confluence in company. My gaze ran clockwise.

Coffee Tent

May 27, 2019
Day 18

Karamoja region. Hours before sunrise, I heard the bulls. Pushing earth. The loosening of soil has a particular smell. I waited for daybreak to exit my tent. Upon unzipping the tent, I witnessed the plowing of these plains. Pairs of bulls under the care and direction of master farmers. Their lines dig strong and resilient. On and on. Back and forth they pass. A woman swung a thick machete and dangled a whip while her newborn baby slept in a sack on her back. A gentleman anchoring the plow with his lean mighty seasoned from the land over time. Old man strength. Hours in the dark before hours in the light. They prepared what is to come. Maize the principal crop. Beans and potatoes follow. How many lives from how many

generations have cultivated this land?
How far back and how far forward will
these lines cut? I am scattered somewhere
on the lines and last night placed around
their campfire, I saw sapphires between
the flickers of the fire - exact qualities
humanity should aspire to be. Qualities
~~that~~ that can cut a plot to season a
soul. They welcomed me ~~warmly~~ with
kindness. Fed me from their labors and
gave warm soil to sleep on. Between the
flames I clearly see.

Ugandan Soil

15. 6. 13

Walking Iceland's Fimmvörðuháls volcanic landscape. Blanketed moss, black ground, ice and snow. Every hour brings all weather conditions. All colors. On the course of weathering, the trail gives. Otherworldly, mind-blowing, landscape of fantasy. Looking up at an ice capped mountaintop in the expanse of the forward landscape, knowing the answer, I spoke up and asked my guide "is that where we are going?" Serious as can be - he responded, "it doesn't matter." Plain and simple, onward is the only choice. Together we took it!

Fimmvörðuháls